Glowing endorsements for *Denied a Chance*

"In the fight for the human right of protection of self and loved ones, Nikki Goeser is 'a hero of the cause' and her murdered husband, Ben, a martyr to the same cause. Her new book *Denied A Chance* is essential reading for anyone who objectively wishes to understand the concealed carry movement and the foremost of human rights, that of self-defense."

– Massad Ayoob
Author of *In the Gravest Extreme*

"Anti-Gun laws and the Restaurant No-Carry laws that some states have create unintended consequences. What happened to Nikki Goeser should not have happened."

– Dick Heller
of Heller vs DC

"Nikki Goeser's story is a testament to the heartbreak of gun control gone wrong. A law that was intended to save lives actually helped kill the love of her life. But Nikki did not just sit in the closet and mourn her loss. Instead, she courageously decided not to suffer in silence. Boldly telling her story to anyone who would listen, Nikki has become a respected voice in the battle for human rights."

– Kathy Jackson
Author of *The Cornered Cat*

Glowing endorsements for *Denied a Chance*

"Nicole Goeser has an important story to tell, and her raw, plainspoken truths should be heard by all. As the gun-control debate rages on and opponents of gun ownership try to portray us as people who care more about their firearms than family, Nicole's dedication and love for her husband proves them all wrong."

– Cam Edwards
Host of *NRA News, Cam & Company*

"Denied the ability to carry her gun for self-defense by the state when she and her husband needed it most, Nikki successfully fought to change the laws in Tennessee in the wake of her husband's brutal murder. Thank God for American Patriots and freedom fighters like Nikki Goeser."

– Mark Walters, Host of Armed American Radio
Author of *Lessons from Armed America*

"As an ode to her beloved husband Ben, Nikki must tell her story … draw strangers, media, and legislators in, and make them understand. It is a job that she did not ask for or desire. It was thrust upon her. And she delivers."

– Suzanna Hupp, Author of
From Luby's to the Legislature:
One Woman's Fight Against Gun Control

Acknowledgments

Mom and Dad, thanks for supporting me and standing by me through some very dark and difficult times. Bow and Susan, I am so lucky to have a brother and sister who actually like me even after I picked on you so much when we were kids. I love you guys so much and thank you for being there to talk to through all this.

Suzanna Gratia Hupp, when I heard the story of your parent's murder it shook me, and I never dreamed I would be faced with something similar one day. Thank you for your encouragement and kindness through a nightmare you know so well.

Dr. John Lott Jr., thank you for all of your time and effort researching the facts and educating the public about the importance of our Second Amendment. You are someone I admire a great deal.

Buford Tune, I can't thank you enough for your support, your firearms training and for speaking at Ben's wake. Officer Williams, I am grateful that you were the officer who took care of me the night I lost Ben. You are a special man.

John Harris, I'll never forget meeting you for the first time at the Tennessee Firearms Association meeting at a time when I was in despair. Thank you for your support of me and for all your work in Tennessee fighting for our right to keep and bear arms.

Senator Doug Jackson, thank you for sponsoring and helping pass a great piece of legislation that gives families the ability to defend themselves in restaurants. Senator, I'm pretty sure Stephen Colbert can't hit a apple pie dead center like you did!

Linda Walker, thanks for all your hard work in Ohio and beyond, letting me crash at your place and taking me shooting.

Dick Heller, thanks for the hugs and phone conversations (thumbs up!).

Barbara Oonk, you have been a great friend and so fun to go shoot with.

Ed Levine, thanks for your friendship and standing up for our rights as Founder of Virginia Open Carry.

Representative Judd Matheny, thank you for standing by your principles and our Constitution instead of politics.

I want to sincerely thank the entire NRA family for helping secure our freedoms and giving American citizens who have been victimized and defenseless a voice to educate others on the importance of the Second Amendment.

Others I want to thank are... The TN Firearms Association, Ohioans for Concealed Carry, Buckeye Firearms Association, Students for Concealed Carry, Virginia Citizens Defense League, Tennessee Gun Owners Association, Gun Owner's of America, Second Amendment Foundation, Representative Danny Bubp, Senator Joe Uecker, The Second Amendment Sisters, Mark Walters of Armed American Radio, Amanda Collins, David Burnett, Skip Coryell, Bill Oliver, Bob and Kathleen Long, The Carlton family, The Bartley family, Chris Cox, Wayne LaPierre, Cam Edwards, John Popp, Cameron Grey, Ginny Simone, Guns and Patriots, American Sheepdog, Mike Piccione.

Last but not least, many thanks to all my wonderful Nashville friends. Without your emotional support and help, getting past all this would have been just about impossible. There is no way to list everyone here, but you know who you are.

Denied

a

Chance

How gun control helped a stalker murder my husband

Nicole
Goeser

Published by White Feather Press. (www.whitefeatherpress. com)

ISBN 978-1-61808-064-6

Printed in the United States of America

Cover design created by Ron Bell of AdVision Design Group (www.advisiondesigngroup.com)

Publisher's note: Some of the names in this book have been changed to protect the privacy of the individuals involved.

White Feather Press

Reaffirming Faith in God, Family, and Country!

Foreword
by Suzanna Hupp

I first met Nikki a few years ago, not in the way people used to meet with a handshake and a smile, but the way so many soul mates are able to find each other in this day and age: through technology.

I spend so much of my time away from husband and kids that during the evenings and weekends I am home I tend to wall off the rest of the world. We do not have a landline telephone anymore, and it is a rare incident indeed for me to answer my cell phone. And text? No way, Jose! Not unless it is with my immediate family or about a horse ... my two real passions. If the phone rings and the screen does not light up with a family member's name, I just let it go to voicemail. If the caller does not leave a message, I feel vindicated that it was not important and would have wasted my precious time. So now you know: on weekends and evenings I really do screen my calls. Don't take it personally.

But for some bizarre reason that Sunday afternoon, I answered the ring. I cannot say that it was accidental. I actually looked down at the number, did not recognize it, and answered it anyway. A young and sweet-sounding voice introduced herself as Nikki Goeser, and after verifying my identity she quickly explained how she had gotten my number and apologized for calling. I really did not know where the conversation was going, but since she had gotten my number from a Second Amendment Sister I assumed she was getting around to inviting me to speak at some engagement or another. There was something in her voice, though, that made me particularly attentive. I could not put a name to it, and she certainly was not crying or exhibiting any other obvious emotion, but there was something.

I moved outside and found a seat in the shade and waited

as she assured herself that she could continue.

For the next half an hour, I sat with a breeze gently moving the porch swing where I sat with the cell phone glued to my ear. This young woman, whom I had never met, with a sweet southern drawl that somehow matched the breeze on my cheek, poured out her soul to a complete stranger via satellite. But she knew that we had a connection that went far beyond the technology, we had shared the violent loss of people we love. And that is an instant, deep and abiding thread that does not contain words or actions … only understanding. Profound understanding.

Time has passed and with it, I have watched Nikki make her way through the "normal" ebb and flow of emotions that come after such a dreadful, and thankfully abnormal event. She has successfully channeled her pain and rage into a cause in the hopes that others might learn from her experience. Have you ever wondered why you will crane your neck when nearing some catastrophic occurrence? It is an interesting phenomenon that people (yes, even legislators) cannot help looking when they drive by an accident, or see tornado damage, or crumbling twin towers. Perhaps it is the "There, but for the Grace of God, go I" feeling that creates an interconnection with the stranger being loaded into the ambulance.

That is now Nikki's job. She must, as an ode to her beloved husband Ben, tell her story and recreate that connection. Draw strangers, media, and legislators in, and make them understand. It is a job that she did not ask for or desire. It was thrust upon her.

And she delivers.

– Suzanna Hupp, Author of
From Luby's to the Legislature:
One Woman's Fight Against Gun Control

To Ben

I was blessed to have you if only for a moment in the span of this life. You taught me about what love really is, how a woman should be treated and made me look forward to my tomorrows. The short time I had with you helped shape who I am today and the decisions I will make for my future. Your love for me and your kindness is something I will always remember and cherish. Your death taught me about true sorrow but in that sorrow I learned even more about love.

"All my possessions ...

for a moment of time."

– Elizabeth I,
Queen of England,
1558 to 1603

CHAPTER I

TODAY WILL BE THE LAST DAY OF my husband's life. Ben and I have been married for 1 year, 4 months and 2 days. Ben has just 16.5 hours left here on this earth with me. Sixteen and a half hours of time and we have no idea the end is coming. Little do we know, the end of our future together is already set in motion.

The clock is ticking.

Ben will be brutally murdered right in front of me tonight by a male acquaintance who I have no idea has been stalking me. I will make the decision to follow an incredibly stupid law of the State of Tennessee and leave my permitted handgun, which my husband bought for me as a birthday gift, locked in my vehicle tonight. Because of that law, I will have no way to defend my husband and he will die in a room full of helpless people.

Instead of blaming the gun like so many other victims of violent crime, I choose to stand for what I know is right.

I take the opposite position and help in a movement of freedom to defend our Second Amendment Rights, so law-abiding citizens can at least have a fighting chance to protect themselves from predators like Ben's murderer – a chance Ben and I were denied. Our story will be told in the United States and abroad as an example of what can happen when law-abiding citizens are disarmed. I recall that old saying "What doesn't kill you, makes you grow stronger," and I am about to find out if it is true.

My life is about to change forever.

ع ع ع

(6:00 AM) MY ALARM CLOCK JUST WENT OFF. MY HUSBAND and I are lying in our bed half awake. Ben was laid off from his job as a Graphics Coordinator a little over a month earlier. This was Thursday, and I recall waking up with an overwhelming desire to stay home from work and be with my husband. I had no idea at the time that this move would give me the opportunity to have those last precious moments with the man I had chosen to spend the rest of my life.

At the time I worked at a vocational college as a financial aid advisor. I advised students on possible financial aid packages for higher education programs they were interested in. Most of the people that came in were very nice and looking for a brighter future. Little did they know, with the state of our economy and today's job market, even with a higher education, they would have to struggle to find work. Chances are, they may have to take a job that is not what they really want to do or they will have to take a part-time job – but like so many Americans, they will do it in order to pay the bills.

It took me almost a year to get this job. I sat in a cubicle day in and day out doing the same repetitive spreadsheets for every tattooed, pierced, name-brand-clothing-wearing young person with a cell phone nicer than mine who walked in the door. Many prospective students even had multiple children and I wondered how they got by with more expenses than I had myself. Many of these young adults were on food stamps and in Section 8 Public Housing. But at least these were young people who cared about their future and wanted a better life and were willing to work for it instead of just remaining on government assistance. I respected that.

The one thing I really enjoyed about the job was the mini seminars I ran for students getting ready to graduate. I talked with them about the financial aid process and repaying their loans, budgeting and using their money wisely once they graduated. I used this opportunity to talk with them about Dave Ramsey and his advice on how to live within your means in his book called *Financial Peace*. I try to live by that book myself, and I wanted them to learn about living debt free and about ways to accomplish that goal. But even though I enjoyed doing this, my mind wandered and I thought of how I had been working in the business world for the past eight years since I graduated college at The University of Tennessee – and how I made only about $3,000 more than I did coming out of college.

I was grateful I had a job but still somewhat jaded by my pay scale. This was not what I had planned on doing career wise. I had hopes of going to graduate school and perhaps advancing myself and taking my psychology degree further by studying forensic psychology or possibly law. Well, as with many people, life happened, bills happened and I did not ever get back in school. I was in my early thirties at the time, and career wise was not where I wanted to be. But Ben … he was the one bright shining part of my life. We were married on New Year's Eve 2007 and I was absolutely head over heels madly in love with my husband, I knew that no matter what happened in my life, whether it be with my career or anything else, I would be okay because I had Ben.

Now, looking back on that morning, lying in bed beside the man I loved, I recalled an overwhelming need to be with Ben that I couldn't shake. So I reasoned with myself and thought, *To heck with it, I'm taking the day off.* My Manager had told me just a few days earlier that I was one of the hardest working employees in his department so why should it be a big deal if I take one little sick day, right?

I tapped Ben on the shoulder and told him I was going to take the day off.

Ben said "Aw Babe, why don't you wait and take a day off when we can actually go somewhere and have fun together? I have to work on Omar's house today and we can't really spend quality time together."

Ben had taken a few odd jobs working on people's homes doing various "fix it" projects to make a little money while he was looking for another corporate job. He'd been working on our friend Omar's house for the past week or so. Omar had a beautiful 1930's brick home in a nice neighborhood, but the house was in need of repair. Ben was asked to replace floors, paint, put in new light fixtures, etc.

I told Ben that I didn't care. I would go with him and help him on the house. I just wanted to be with him. He agreed as he grinned. I called in sick but felt really uncomfortable fibbing to my boss like that.

Looking back now, I am so very glad I did.

ع ع ع

It looked like it was going to be a beautiful day. Bright and sunny with a slight breeze. We headed down the road in

4

Ben's old pickup truck to grab some breakfast first. We then stopped by Habitat for Humanity where we bought everything we needed to fix up Omar's house. Flooring, spackle, paint, light fixtures and fans were all on our list. We purchased everything we needed at a steal of a deal and would be reimbursed plus labor cost once the job was finished in a few weeks. Ben called Omar while we were on the way to his house (Omar was at work) and told him that I had taken the day off to be with him.

Omar had known Ben for several years before I started dating him. They met at the Karaoke Restaurant and were like peas and carrots, literally. They were always out singing somewhere together and wherever you found Omar, you found Ben also. They were best buds. Omar and I became friends once Ben and I started dating and he won me over with his great sense of humor: a little sick and demented but hilarious! Ben was so excited about me taking the day off, he started yelling in the phone about it and I could hear Omar saying … "Oh God, you two lovebirds make me sick! You had better not 'do it' in my house you two!"

Omar is a true entertainer. Picture the pianist/singer Jerry Lee Lewis with red hair and you have Omar. Omar worked for a law firm during the day but at night his favorite thing to do after work was sing at the various karaoke restaurants in downtown Nashville. Omar and Ben would escape the everyday grind at the office for years by meeting for some karaoke fun on a regular basis. Omar had been on the show *Star Search* back in the 1980s hosted by Ed McMahon and was a very talented singer.

Omar spent years and years as a wedding singer but he really belonged on Broadway. He was always entertaining the tourists that came into the Nashville restaurants with songs like *Wave on Wave*, *Walking in Memphis*, *Somewhere over the Rainbow*, and they all LOVED him. Nashville is full of talent and sadly many dreams are busted in this town by the sheer magnitude of competition. The karaoke restaurant was one place where many of these local golden voices would meet after the stresses of a long work day.

؏ ؏ ؏

WE GOT TO OMAR'S AND WENT TO WORK. BEN WAS UP IN THE attic cutting a hole in the floor to install a fan in the ceiling of a lower bathroom. I was in the dining room ripping up old flooring. We teased each other throughout the day telling jokes or getting sidetracked with a kiss here and there. It was hard work but it was fun as we both loved just being together. We worked on various projects around the house all day.

Around 5:00 pm dark clouds were setting in outside and we heard a weather siren going off close to the neighborhood as it began to rain. We walked out onto Omar's front porch to look at the storm that was rolling in. The wind was picking up and we both just looked at each other and realized we'd better get home. We knew we had a karaoke show to run that night at Jonny's Sports Bar and we had to get ready. Ben had decided he wanted to purchase a mobile karaoke system and try running shows as a side job about a year prior. We had been running karaoke shows at night for almost a year for a little grocery and gas money. So we hopped in Ben's truck and on the way home we stopped by Sonic for Cherry Lime-Aids (our favorite).

On the way home Ben talked about one of his friends whose wife had died from cancer several years ago. They had been married for thirty-plus years. They were crazy about each other all those years, and he had taken care of her up until her last breath. A female co-worker comforted this widower in his grief of losing his wife and he ended up marrying her. Ben told me how his friend had re-married too soon and not under the right circumstances and he was not exactly "happy" with the way things were.

She was nowhere near as understanding or kind as his first wife, and they did not have a genuine closeness like the marriage he'd previously had. He was still grieving for his deceased wife even though he was re-married, and no longer felt he could verbalize that sense of loss to his current wife. Ben told me that should anything ever happen to him, he would want me to move on but he would want me to be with someone who put me first and truly loved me.

I look back on this conversation that my husband and I shared that day and it perplexes me that we had such a discussion. Getting to spend this last day with my husband and having this conversation has helped me deal with losing him and has provided perspective on what type of person it will take to share a life with me in my future.

Ben and I traveled on a cruise for our one-year anniversary. Here we are at the Port of Miami.

Ben has 4 hours left to live ...

WE GOT HOME AND BEN KISSED ME AS SOON AS WE GOT OUT OF his Chevy pickup truck. Ben and I got ready to go run another Thursday night of karaoke fun at Jonny's Sports Bar. We had not been there in three weeks due to some sort of fight night or sports event they'd substituted on what were normally karaoke nights. I'll never forget the rain coming down that evening. It was coming down at a steady pace and I remember asking Ben, as he started loading up our very heavy equipment in the Jeep, whether he would consider calling the sports bar and asking them if we could take a rain check. I was concerned our equipment would get ruined in the pouring rain as we had never purchased protective covers. I said, "Babe, we could just fix dinner and put on our PJ's and watch a movie together tonight."

Ben just looked at me while he got some garbage bags to put over the speakers and said "Now Nik, we have an obligation to these folks, we need to go and run this show like we said we would." I was also getting kind of tired of dealing with drunks on karaoke nights. The past three weeks of not working at Jonny's had not broken my heart at all. It was difficult going to bed at 2:00 am after working at the sports bar and then waking up at 6:00 am to go to my job at the college. But I knew Ben was right and began to help him load up the equipment. As I look back on that night, I wish I'd put up more resistance.

It was about a ten-minute drive for us out to the sports bar from our home. We parked our vehicle in front and started our regular Thursday night routine of moving everything into the restaurant. We would always get there at around 8:00

pm to eat first, as part of our agreement was that Jonny's would let us eat for free. That was fair, as we did not charge them anywhere near what other karaoke hosts charged. Our shows ran from 9:00 pm till midnight but sometimes until one o'clock in the morning, depending on the crowd. Ben LOVED karaoke and he got a kick out of watching talented singers or people making fools of themselves. I LIKED karaoke and could enjoy it most times when there were not too many inconsiderate drunks being difficult.

Ben and I finished our dinner and we started running the show at 9:00 pm on the dot. We always started the night off with me singing the first song so that Ben could tweak the microphones. Our microphones (that cost an arm and a leg) could make singers sound better than they really were but only after some adjusting.

The restaurant was busy and people were happy and singing along to their favorite songs. We always had a very long list of singers and sometimes customers would get impatient waiting their turn. But it was the people who seemed to drink the most who were the most impatient, and the most willing to throw down a twenty-dollar bill to have their name moved up the song list. I'd think to myself, *buddy … you should save that money to pay for a cab ride home!*

This particular night looked like it was going to be pretty fun … until 10:30 pm rolled around.

"We understand death for the first time when he puts his hand upon one whom we love."

– Madame de Stael

1776 – 1817

CHAPTER 2

The Nightmare Begins

AN HOUR AND A HALF INTO THE karaoke show, I was standing up at our laptop computer typing in songs for customers. This eerie feeling came over me as I looked up and noticed a man in the crowd that Ben had previously asked to leave me alone about a month ago. He was standing there by himself staring right through me. This man had been a karaoke customer of mine when I worked downtown at various karaoke restaurants hosting shows. To the best of my memory, he showed up on Nashville's karaoke scene around September or October of 2008. He just blended with the crowd and was pretty ordinary.

He was a pudgy, five-foot-four fellow with a brown mustache. He would usually wear a cowboy hat or baseball cap. The typical cowboy-wanna-be type that frequently roams around the streets of downtown Nashville. We thought he was just a tourist at first. A few times he would get up to sing and tell me "This song is just for you." Of course, like some people that come to Nashville thinking they will make it in the music business, this guy could not sing. He started coming into the BuckWild Saloon often and we realized he must live here. Ben always took it upon himself to act as an informal welcoming committee to those "newbies" that showed up. My husband was well loved at the work place – fun, jovial, optimistic, lighthearted and always smiling. The girls I worked with at the karaoke venues all loved Ben and would hug his neck the second he walked in the door. Ben was always welcoming new people and befriending them. My husband introduced the man who would end up murdering him casually around the room with the regulars.

I was more reserved with people I did not know well. I do not ever remember having an actual face-to-face conversation with this man, other than "Hi, how are you doing? Are you having a good time tonight. Good to see you and thanks for the tip." There was one time when this man actually gave me a $100 tip. I thought he'd made a mistake so I took it back to him and thanked him just to make sure. I could tell by the smirk on his face that it was no accident. He then found me after that on Myspace and sent me a friend request.

At the time, I just thought he was a little awkward and added him like I do the other customers. People from all over the world come to see Nashville and inevitably there will be some oddballs. He sent me a few messages that were completely normal as a customer and I responded politely. Then around the holidays of 2008 he started getting a little more brazen. Still, the messages did not throw any red flags because he was simply saying I was attractive. Men in the bar say that to women and we say thanks and smile and move on doing our job.

He then started sending me messages that were inappropriate over Myspace, and I ended up deleting him and blocking him. One message said maybe I should consider leaving my husband, that Ben was perhaps too old for me, and asked if I ever wanted children. He wrote that he'd had to break it off with someone who really loved him once; it was difficult to do, but sometimes you just have to do what needs to be done.

I responded by letting him know that what he was saying to me was inappropriate and that I was happily married. I showed this message to my husband. Ben thought it was weird and said, "that guy must have a crush on you." Ben and I both blew it off. I did not delete the guy right away because I have been hit on before by guys at the bar and I just have to tell them no. They move on, trying to catch the next fish in the sea. No big deal.

This man then sent me a hateful message back basically trying to break me down and make fun of my physical appearance (the exact opposite of what he had been saying). In the message, he told me that he disliked my profile picture because it printed out like a postage stamp. I had no idea what in the heck that was supposed to mean other than it freaked me out that he was apparently printing my picture. It was at this point that I realized that "this guy ain't right."

I showed this message to Ben as well and we both agreed that this man needed to be deleted. I did not respond to his last message. I deleted him and blocked him from having any access to my profile. He showed up about two weeks later at one of the karaoke shows I was running at a saloon in downtown Nashville. He just sat there and stared at me the whole time. Unlike other times he had come in before, he did not sing. Ben was in the crowd with our friends enjoying the night when this man came up to Ben and asked him how he was doing, like he had never sent the strange messages to me and all was well.

Ben was never a fighter or instigator but would stand up for me if need be. Ben just looked at him and said, "Look, I read the messages that you sent my wife and I read what you said about me. You're scaring her. Please leave my wife alone." This man then declared that the messages were actually from a crazy ex girlfriend of his who somehow knew how to hack into his Myspace account. "It wasn't me" he professed. Of course Ben did not buy this phony story and just brushed it off and said "Okay, whatever." Ben joined our crowd of friends again and he proceeded to tell me of this conversation that took place while we made our way home that night.

This same man came into the same restaurant one more time a few weeks later. He stood in the crowd and stared at me while I was on stage running the show. I went around the crowd with my tip jar like I normally did at various points throughout the night. I noticed out of the corner of my eye that he had money in his hand. I walked right past him, did not stop, did not look at him or acknowledge him in any way. I simply wanted him to go away and leave me alone. Everyone was talking, drinking and having a good time around him but he was just standing there still looking at me. After the next song, he left.

ۼ ۼ ۼ

We had not seen this man in a solid month since then and now he was here at Jonny's Sports Bar, where I had never seen him before. This restaurant is nowhere near downtown, where this man normally goes for karaoke nights, and Ben already asked him to leave me alone. So what was he doing here? This cannot be good. This restaurant is a good 35-minute drive from downtown! This guy had gone way out of his way to come here … and for what? It was at this point that I realized this man was not simply a dedicated karaoke customer. This guy did not just have a simple crush on me. This man was actually stalking me. I remember feeling annoyed and concerned by his presence. This man had never exhibited any signs of violence but he made me feel very uneasy. He had never threatened me but he was just plum weird, a loner, awkward and socially stunted. He just kept staring right at me. Something was telling me to get this guy out of here and quick.

I noticed he had on a tan Carhartt jacket and a camouflage ball cap. He was standing there near the entrance staring right at me with that same weird smirk on his face as all the other times. I made a mental note of where he was in the crowd and then turned to my husband who was sitting at a table behind me. I told Ben, "He is here, you know … that man that sent me the strange messages over Myspace." Ben looked up and saw him and acknowledged his presence. I said, "Ben honey I don't feel comfortable at all with that man being here, I am going to ask management to remove him." Ben agreed with me and said, "Okay Babe, do whatever you need to do."

I went back up to the computer to get the next singer up, as I wanted to keep the show going and not let this man see that I was up to anything. I turned to look back at Ben and was shocked to see this man had somehow walked around behind me when I was working on the computer and sat right next to Ben at his table. This had me concerned and I looked straight at Ben to see if there was any distress on his face. My stalker was talking to Ben about something, but whatever it was had to be normal and not a heated discussion because Ben seemed totally relaxed. Ben just gave me a look like "Heck Nik, I have no clue why he is sitting here trying to talk to me." I learned later from the detective, that my stalker had said he was telling Ben "how nice my hair looked."

I walked to the back hallway and grabbed the manager, Jackie. I instructed her to follow me, and I let her know I was very concerned and needed to speak with her. I lead her through the back kitchen and out the door into the other side of the restaurant's dining room. I stayed hidden beside a brick wall so my stalker couldn't see me. I told Jackie that the man sitting next to my husband at the table was stalking me, that I didn't feel comfortable and I needed him to be removed. I told her exactly what he had on and described what he looked like. She looked around the corner and said "Nikki, there is nobody sitting next to Ben." I peeked out and noticed that my stalker was gone. I told Jackie to stay there and I would be right back.

I walked back around through the kitchen to the other side of the restaurant where Ben was still sitting at the table in the dining room and asked him where the man had gone. Ben pointed and said that he had gone to the restroom in the back. I looked that way and looked around the crowd to see if he was anywhere out there. I was not positive he was in the restroom even if he had indicated that to Ben. I kissed my husband on the cheek and went back to where I had left Jackie waiting.

She said, "Did he go to the bathroom?" "Yes," I said. Jackie then told me not to worry, they would handle it as soon as he got out. I then saw my husband get up from the table and go to our computer to keep the show going, as I was no longer there.

My stalker came out of the restroom and stood several feet behind Ben in a doorway that entered into the pool table room. Ben was typing in songs and Jackie had grabbed a barback (her boyfriend) and they were walking across the room to confront my stalker. Something told me not to move and not to get involved. That little voice in your head that we all have was telling me, Nikki stay put. I knew I had no real way to defend us if need be. This guy freaked me out and I knew he could possibly be trouble, I just had no idea how much trouble. Realizing I was being stalked, I did the only thing I could at the time, stay hidden, inform management of the situation and have management remove him.

I knew my gun was locked in my vehicle. It was illegal to bring it in the restaurant, because they served alcohol, even though I was permitted to carry it for self-defense. I stayed beside that brick wall about twenty feet away, but could see everything going on out in front of me in the dining room. My stalker had no clue where I was. I saw him standing several feet behind Ben and looking around the room as if he was looking for someone. I assumed he was looking for me as I tried to stay hidden beside the brick wall. My stalker continued to just stand behind Ben loitering and looking around acting anxious.

I could see my husband was busy on the computer, and Jackie started talking to my stalker who was still standing several feet behind Ben. Ben had no idea that any of this was going on behind him as he worked on the computer. I could tell they were asking my stalker to leave and he did not want to comply. He took a few steps backwards, started unzipping his jacket, reached for something under his arm and pulled out a .45 caliber semi-auto handgun. At this very moment I thought to myself in a flicker of a second, *Oh my God, I don't have my gun! He is going to shoot somebody and I don't have my gun!* A waitress standing next to me who was watching grabbed my arm and gasped.

ξ ξ ξ

I REMEMBER THE LIGHTS REFLECTING OFF THE METAL SLIDE OF the gun. He lowered the gun to my husband's head at arm's length as Ben turned around and saw him and tried to duck his aim. The roar of gunfire filled the room. Ben fell to the floor. People started screaming and scattering trying to get out of the restaurant. My stalker then stood over Ben and continued to fire five more rounds into my husband. I was watching this in complete horror, disbelief and helplessness. He very calmly put the gun back in his jacket and walked through the door into the pool table room like he was just going to walk right out of the restaurant without anyone knowing he was the shooter.

As soon as he turned the corner brick wall into that pool table room and there was a barrier between us, I ran to get to my husband. I did not learn until later that Ben's killer had been tackled as soon as he turned that corner by a United States Marine "Todd" who happened to be in the crowd, saw everything, and knew he was the gunman. A group of men formed a pyramid on top of the shooter while Todd took the gun from him. The murder weapon was taken to the back office and secured.

The barback started kicking at Ben's murderer trying to hit him in the face until Todd told him to stop. Men surrounded Ben's murderer and held on to him until the police arrived. Todd may have very well saved my life that night as it would have been very easy for Ben's killer to pop around that corner once I got to Ben and shoot me also.

Ben was lying on his left side facing away from me as I approached him. I was praying that he was still alive. A few people ran up with me and we turned him over on his back. It was at that very moment that the room and what was going on faded out and I realized my husband was dead. There was blood all around my husband's head. I knelt beside him and

I just remember hearing screaming.

I wanted to hold him but I knew this was a crime scene and I couldn't or it could taint the evidence. I just kept my hands on my husband as much as I could and I guess at that point my mind started playing tricks on me. I thought I could see a slight movement. I did not know CPR at the time so I just screamed for someone to help. I was mad at myself that I didn't know how to give CPR and someone else had to do it for Ben. There was a young man there who was a regular on karaoke nights that everyone referred to as "Storm." He started CPR on Ben but after two or three tries he stopped. I begged him not to stop but he just looked at me and said "Nikki, he's been shot in the head, he's gone, nobody can do anything for him, he's gone, I'm sorry."

I remember people grabbing at me and pulling me away from Ben. Now, looking back, I am sure I was a complete basket case and very hard to handle. As I was pulled away once, I remember seeing different faces in front of me saying, "Pray for him, that is all you can do now" and "He is in a better place," and "Was that your husband? Oh, I am so sorry," or "There is nothing you can do for him now. He is in Heaven." Others said, "Screaming is not going to help anything ma'am. Calm Down," or "He is in the Lord's hands."

The room was spinning as I saw these faces and I could feel my own heartbeat in my head. I remember being so confused and angry, telling people to "let me go" and "don't touch me" as I threw myself back on the floor next to Ben. There were two or three men that knelt down around Ben and were trying to talk to me and I suppose trying to calm me down.

Then, after what seemed like an eternity, the police arrived. I have been told they arrived within three minutes of the 911 call, but when it's happening to yourself, it feels like forever. One police officer came in and turned the corner where Ben and I were on the floor and he made eye contact with me. I told him, "This is my husband." I stayed at Ben's side as long as I could until the police told me they had to secure the crime scene. I remember standing up and then seeing Ben's killer with an Officer beside him as he was being handcuffed in the pool table room. I started screaming, "That's him! That's the man that killed my husband!" I lunged toward him but someone grabbed me. If I could have gotten my hands on him at that moment I would have done everything in my power to kill him.

I remember being grabbed from behind and an officer yelling, "Lady! You have got to calm down!" I was lead to the back hallway as my mind twisted with confusion and anger. I did not have the strength to stand or sit up in a chair. All I could do was sit on the floor as Ben's killer was lead away by police. They started putting up crime scene tape around the dining room where my husband's body lay in a pool of his own blood. I just sat there in that hallway with one of the servers sitting next to me as she talked and told me everything was going to be okay. I kept thinking to myself, *How is everything going to be okay? I am never going to get to see my husband again. How could this have happened to us? This cannot be real; this happens to people I see on the news, not us!*

I looked at my hands and it was at this point I realized I had Ben's blood all over my jeans and my hands. The woman next to me said, "Oh honey, let me take you in the bathroom and we will get you cleaned up." With her help, I got in front of the sink and washed my hands. Everything started changing to slow motion as I watched my husband's blood run down the sink and into the drain. I felt like I was going to pass out. I was then taken back to the kitchen by law enforcement.

I sat on the kitchen floor trying to grasp what had just happened. Someone brought me my phone. I ended up on the line with my dad, hysterical to the point that the phone had to be handed off to an officer so my dad could make out what was going on. Someone told me, "Your dad says he is on his way but is in another state." A regular patron of the restaurant named Steve took my cell phone and asked what friends he could call for me. I told him my friend Bobby. Bobby was a firearms training volunteer at the same range I also volunteered at.

Bobby did not answer his phone after several tries so Steve tried my friend Kimberly. Kimberly was a karaoke jockey as well and we both worked at the same restaurant downtown on various nights. Kimberly answered and Steve told her she needed to come to Jonny's Sports Bar right away, because there had been an accident with Ben and he had been shot. I later learned from Kimberly that she had no idea Ben had been killed but thought he was being taken to a hospital.

She called my cell phone back after thinking about it and when Steve answered, Kimberly asked, "Why am I not going to the hospital? If Ben has been shot then won't Nikki and Ben be going to the hospital?" It was at this point that Steve had to break the news to her that "Ben is dead." Kimberly lost it and started crying as she drove. When she pulled herself together, she called our mutual friends Pam and Taylor to inform them of what had happened as she was making her way to the restaurant. Because this happened the day after April Fools' Day, Pam and Taylor thought this was some kind of a sick joke as they made their way to the Sports Bar. It wasn't until they saw the blue lights and yellow tape when they realized this was very real.

Meanwhile, I still sat in that kitchen trying to understand

the unthinkable. There was a group of officers behind me talking in the doorway. They had one young officer guarding the opposite door that went into the crime scene. The owner of Jonny's Sports Bar walked into the kitchen, barely looked down at me and walked past me to speak with the officers in the doorway. The manager, Jackie, sat next to me on the floor as she too tried to grasp what had just happened. I looked down at my jeans and saw Ben's blood. I was now having a very difficult time breathing and asked someone to please get a paramedic for me. I was seriously feeling like I might pass out at any moment. My heart was racing and my chest felt heavy. I began thinking about the possibility that Ben's killer may have figured out where we live and may have gone to our home first to find us and may have killed our dogs. Violent stalkers have been known to do horrible things to animals who belong to the person they are stalking. I asked an officer to send a patrol car out to our home to check on our dogs. They later called in to let me know that our dogs were fine.

I then saw my friend, Kimberly, enter the room along with a detective. I told Kimberly who the shooter was as she sat on the floor with me. Kimberly said, "Oh my God!" and the detective said, "Ma'am, so you know the person that did this?" I told him, "Yes, he was a karaoke customer of mine and he was stalking me." Kimberly said, "I know this guy too, he was a karaoke customer of mine as well and he had sent me strange messages also." The detective let us both know he would need us down at the south precinct so they could get more details.

It was at this point that the paramedics arrived and put me on a gurney. I remember being scared out of my mind to go out that back kitchen door on this rolling bed, convinced that the shooter had an accomplice waiting out there to pop me off too. I asked an officer to walk beside the bed, as I was

24

loaded up in the ambulance. I even asked the EMT if the glass in the ambulance was bullet proof. I was scared like I have never been scared before. They assured me I would be okay. A patrol car followed the ambulance I was in. I was taken to a hospital where they evaluated me for shock. A chaplain officer came into my room in the ER and the officer that followed behind my ambulance came in and sat next to my bed.

This officer's name is Brian Williams and he was the officer that first came in and locked eyes with me while I was kneeling next to Ben on the restaurant floor. After Ben's death, this officer ended up becoming a friend of mine. He is a wonderful person and I was very lucky to have him with me that horrible night.

Officer Williams just sat there somber next to me as I asked him several questions. I asked him if he was married. I suppose at the time I was trying to connect with someone who was married and could understand the loss I was feeling. He told me, "Yes, I am," as he showed me his wedding band. He told me about his wife and his two little children and showed me pictures in his wallet. I asked him, "If someone murdered your wife or one of your children right in front of you, what would you do and how would you feel?" He simply said, "It would be horrible and I can only imagine how you feel right now." Kimberly, Pam and Taylor showed up at the hospital and stayed in the room with me while I was being checked by the nursing staff. Kimberly and Pam were talking about how this same man said strange things to them and made them feel uncomfortable also.

I was then taken by Officer Williams to the south precinct where the police could get details from all of us about this man. I was walked down a hallway, and the first thing I noticed was a chair sitting in the hallway with the murderer's tan Carhartt jacket and the camouflage baseball cap he had on at the restaurant. I knew they had to have him in there nearby and I panicked yelling, "He's here! Oh my god he's here and I am getting out of here! I'm not doing this!"

I started to back away but I was grabbed by my friends and assured by the officers that he was not there and that it was going to be okay. An officer then grabbed the jacket and hat and took them out of my sight. At the time, I could not understand why in the world they would have his things in the hallway for me to see. Looking back now, I suppose it was a tactic to just re-affirm that I knew exactly who the shooter was. I was taken into an interrogation room with my friends where we talked about this man who had just taken my husband from me.

The first thing the detective asked me was "Do you remember talking to me in the restaurant?" I looked at him trying to remember him but I couldn't. I could only recognize the symbol on his shirt. He said, "Well then, you are doing better than most." I told him everything I knew and my friends Kimberly and Pam talked to him as well. I sat there thinking, *Why am I not crying?* I must have said it out loud because I remember someone saying, "You are in shock." I sat there just numb. I can tell anyone reading this that it's not like what they show in movies where someone goes through something horribly traumatic and starts crying right away. You want to and need to, but you are literally so overwhelmed that your body takes over to help you cope and you become numb. I was numb for hours.

ۼ ۼ ۼ

OFFICER WILLIAMS THEN DROVE ME BACK TO JONNY'S SPORTS Bar. The parking lot was completely empty except for one vehicle – my own. There my Jeep sat, parked just where Ben had left it about seven hours before. My little sister, Susan, had just arrived from Kentucky. My Dad had called her and given her the news and my whereabouts. My sister's boyfriend was with her and would drive my Jeep back to my house and Officer Williams would drive me back in his patrol car. I had explained to the officer that I was a right-to-carry permit holder and I had my gun locked in my vehicle. I told him that I needed to get my gun out of my Jeep and secure it in my purse because Susan's boyfriend is not a permit holder and by the very nature of our state law, if he were to drive my vehicle, he would be in possession of a gun illegally. Officer Williams seemed very hesitant to let me go get my gun out of the console. I know he must have been thinking, *Okay ... this woman has just witnessed her husband murdered and I am not real sure what her frame of mind is right now. Will she try to kill herself with the gun?*

I could tell by the look on his face that this was what he was concerned about. So I just said "Officer, I can understand why you are concerned. If it would make you feel better, you can get the gun and secure it yourself. But I have to get the gun out of my Jeep."

Officer Williams very hesitantly agreed. I proceeded to get my Smith and Wesson .38 caliber Airweight revolver out of the console and put it in my purse. The officer secured my purse in his trunk. As he was driving, I spoke with him about gun rights and the law and how helpless I felt and how upset I was. I talked about Ben and our marriage and God. As we pulled into the driveway I asked him if he would check the property completely to make sure it was safe. So he checked every room and walked around the house. I showed him pictures of Ben and I in our family room. I wanted him to see what Ben looked like happy and living instead of what he and I had seen tonight in that restaurant. It was important to me for him to see that Ben was not just some dead body; this was my life, my husband.

27

I looked at the clock, and it was about 4:00 am. Susan and her boyfriend came in and Officer Williams gave me a hug. "Ma'am, I am so sorry," he said before leaving. I sat on the floor of my family room and I was able to cry now. You can probably imagine how bad it was. I have never cried so hard in my life. My sister did what she could to console me, but I could tell she did not know what in the heck to do or what to say. What do you say to someone like me at a time like this? Other than losing a child, this is a married couple's worst nightmare and I was living it. The nurses at the hospital had given me a prescription for an anti-anxiety drug called Lorazepam. I took my first pill. If it were not for this medication, I don't think I would have been able to control my emotions, plan my husband's funeral and deal with the huge crowd of people that were soon headed my way.

"I felt like a walking zombie. I had no real concept of time and just remember many people coming and going."

CHAPTER 3

The Day After

I WAS NOW A WIDOW AT THE AGE OF thirty-three. The harder I tried to stop crying, the more the tears came. I had never lost anyone that was really close to me before. I would never be able to hold my husband again. I would never hear him say "Nik, I love you." I would never again receive the love letters he surprised me with every month. I would never spend nights talking with my husband about anything and everything and enjoying that boisterous laugh of his. Ben would no longer be here to offer me his shoulder or ear when I had a hard time. The little things I sometimes took for granted that he helped me with would now be mine alone to bear.

Had I not been disarmed, I could have had the chance to save Ben. The choices I would have made would most likely have been different had I been armed. I kept seeing Ben die over and over again in my mind. I was reliving everything and feeling horribly guilty. I thought of the events that transpired and the different scenarios that could have taken place or decisions I would have made if I'd had my gun. Every scenario lead me to stopping Ben's killer. I thought about the training I had been through before getting my handgun carry permit, going through intermediate firearms training and volunteering at the range for armed guard training and permit training. I will never know if that training would have been useful.

I just sat there, my mind overwhelmed with these thoughts. I was still in total shock. When you are in shock you have no real sense of time so I have no idea how long I sat in my bedroom crying. (I have been told it was many hours.) My sister was in the family room with her boyfriend and I could hear them on the phone with my father and then talking to my mother later. Susan would come into the room and check on me but she had no idea what to do and she started crying herself while on the phone with one of her friends. My sister took over my cell phone and talked to mine and Ben's friends who had been calling because some saw the story on the news. Word was quickly spreading. She did her best to let them know what had happened. I did not want to speak to anyone. A few people called and asked if what they heard was some kind of a joke.

I walked over to my husband's closet and opened the door, sat down on the floor and just stared at his clothes hanging where he had last put them. With every shirt I saw a memory of when and where he had worn it. The black jersey T-shirt with holes and rips in it was the one Ben would wear all the time when he was working on the house outside in the mornings, mowing or fixing things around our property.

The brown-striped button-down dress shirt was the one I bought him for his birthday, and he wore it to a Christmas party we ran karaoke for. My husband had a love for funny T-shirts. He had a Camouflage shirt that had the words "You can't see me" on the front and his bright red T-shirt with a huge heart on the front that said, "I have a heart on for you." I saw the grey T-shirt I bought for him with a cartoon fire hydrant character on it that said, "I put out." My husband had a really great sense of humor and he loved wearing that humor around.

I saw the black Mozart T-shirt that Ben had given his father years ago. When Ben's father, Joseph Goeser, whom we called "Ted," passed away at the age of 93 on December 7, 2008, Ben got the shirt back and wore it often. I pondered on that Mozart shirt for a long time as I sat on the floor. Ben's father was a bright and witty character who was bedridden in his old age but his mind was still sharp. Ben and I would go visit with him in Coconut Grove, Florida and spend hours talking to him in his bedroom. Ted spoke German, French, Spanish and English fluently and always had great stories to tell.

Ted was wearing this Mozart shirt when he told me that he was an interpreter/translator for the Nuremberg Trials in the mid to late 1940s where the major Nazi War Criminals were convicted and sentenced for the mass murder of millions of Jews. He is listed in the records of interpreters as Joseph Edmond Goeser. Ted told me that day how he had lived in Germany as a young boy and traveled as a young adult all over Europe and how he met Ben's mother, Apple Vail, while in Paris, France.

Ben and Ted told me Apple's mother (Ben's grandmother) is famously known in the literary community as the well-known author, Kay Boyle. Ben's grandmother, Kay, wrote many books including *Death of a Man*, published in 1936, a novel that attacked Nazism before most Americans were aware it was a problem. I remembered how Ben said he did not see his grandmother all that much growing up, as she was very politically active and a professor at San Francisco State University. This Mozart shirt made me think of those conversations with Ben and Ted. I decided to put it on. I put on Ben's favorite ripped up old paint-splattered blue jeans that fell around my hips and sat back down on the floor still staring into his closet.

Ben proposed to me in Nashville, Tennessee. It was one of the happiest days of my life.

Then there was a knock at the front door. It was Kimberly. I answered the door and Kimberly grabbed me and hugged me. She helped me get funeral arrangements together and we made notes on everything that needed to be done for Ben. We had to stop at various times as we both were struggling and had to take some time to talk about what happened and to cry.

Later in the morning, my friends Pam and Taylor came over and made breakfast for everyone. I tried to eat but the scrambled eggs that Taylor made reminded me of things I saw less than 24 hours ago and I had to excuse myself while I went to the bathroom to throw up. I simply could not eat. It was a sweet gesture but there was no way I could hold it down. I thought to myself, *Ben can't eat. Ben can't breathe. Ben can't do any of this.* I felt guilty about even taking a sip of water. I ended up losing thirty pounds within four months of Ben's death.

Soon, more people started showing up. My brother, my mom, my dad, my friends from out of town, our karaoke friends (including the now famous Meghan and Josh from *Steel Magnolia*.) Ben had always told them that if they ever made it big, he wanted to be their tour bus driver. They had been performing on the show, *Can you Duet,* at the Wildhorse Saloon in downtown Nashville, but came to the house as soon as they heard what had happened.

Ben and Meghan had been friends for several years, and Meghan and I worked at the same karaoke restaurant running shows. Bless Josh's heart, he was always broke back then. I remember Josh would give me a whole one-dollar tip and then wink at me to move his name up the karaoke song list. I always moved him up, because he was a sweetheart and he put on a great performance. Meghan and Josh ended up winning on *Can You Duet* and got a record deal with Taylor Swift's manager. They are best known for their hit song *Keep on Loving You*. I get choked up hearing them on the radio now or seeing their music videos on Country Music Television. If he was still alive, Ben would be so proud of them.

I could not believe it when both my parents showed up at the house. My parents had not spoken to one another since they divorced when I was fifteen years old. Every holiday, my brother, sister and I would have to make a decision on who we would go see for what holiday. It was a pain in the rear end and it has bothered me all these years that my parents would not have anything to do with each other. Well, that was until Ben was killed. For the first time since I was fifteen, my mother and father were in the same room and they both hugged me at the same time. My house was now full of people.

The medication I was on started to kick in and I felt like a walking zombie. I had no real concept of time and just remember many people coming and going. There were many condolences, flowers and tons of food being delivered. There was enough food for an entire army. And, well, there was pretty much an entire army at my home for the next week. I didn't touch the food, the thought of eating made me want to puke.

Some beautiful white flowers came from the Big Brothers Big Sisters organization. Ben was a "Big Brother" for a ten-year boy by the name of Trent. Ben thought the world of him. Trent's father was in prison and Ben was a positive male figure for him while his father was serving time. Ben would take Trent bowling, to the arcade, putt-putt-golfing, to the movies, four-wheeling, or we would have him over to the house for dinner. I found out from Trent's mother that he learned of Ben's death on the news that next day. His mom told me Trent started screaming and crying when he saw Ben's picture come up on the screen. He ran into the next room and told his mom Ben was dead and it was on television. Trent's mother saw that he received some psychological counseling to deal with Ben's murder. Ben's murderer gave no mind to just how many people's lives he would be affecting.

Kimberly's little five-year-old boy, Ethan, came over to the house with his mother and she had explained to him in very simple terms that Ben went to heaven. Ben and I would baby-sit Ethan often, and when Ethan entered our bedroom and saw Ben's shoes on the floor just where he had left them, Ethan had a puzzled look on his face and said in his little voice, "Nikki, isn't Ben gonna need his shoes in Heaven?" I got choked up. What was I going to tell him? I did not know what to say as I don't have children and I am not skilled in the art of explaining things in kid terms. So I just made something up which was probably enhanced by the drug I was on. I told Ethan that in heaven you can just think of having a pair of shoes and they will magically appear on your feet and you can have any color you want and you can change colors anytime you want and all you have to do is think it. Heck, it sounded good to me and it was a happy thought. I just hoped his Mom was okay with that imaginary, colorful and drug-induced explanation.

I walked around the house looking at pictures of Ben as people watched me and looked concerned. I did not care what anyone thought. I was just trying to hold on to Ben as best as I could. I put his cologne on, his slippers on, I replayed the voicemail he had left me on my cell phone just two days before over and over again. I replayed our engagement video on my computer over and over again. It was as close as I could get to him now.

I still had my husband's blood under my fingernails and tried as best I could to clean myself up before going to the funeral home. My friends and family came along to help. I kept thinking of how Ben's body was in a cold morgue somewhere and how unreal this all seemed to me even though I had witnessed everything happen. I had to make sure Ben's wishes were carried out, and I had to pull myself together to get all of this done.

A news crew came out to the funeral home that day. I was there trying to make arrangements for Ben and they wanted an interview. What is crazy is that I actually went outside and spoke with them. I had no business doing that interview in the kind of shape I was in. I looked horrible as I had cried until there were no more tears and I had not slept at all. When the report aired they had a few clips of me talking about what happened, but they didn't focus much on what I had to say about our Second Amendment and not being able to protect Ben because of the laws. This made me upset as I felt it was important for the public to hear and understand.

Ben wished to be cremated and have his ashes spread in his favorite places. I only had close family and a few of Ben's best friends see his body for closure purposes the first day at the funeral home. I would never want the job of fixing up dead people to look good but somebody has to do it and whoever worked on my husband did an incredible job. Ben simply looked as if he was sleeping, and the entry wound just above his right ear and exit wound was barely noticeable. Though I used to think this was creepy and you may still think so, I found that for those who lose a loved one, this act of closure is very important. The funeral home ended up being packed for the gathering of friends/wake the next day. Nearly three-hundred people showed up.

I had now been driven mentally into "get this taken care of" mode. I literally had to almost be in denial and pretend that this was not my life in order to pull through. I had to shut off wife mode and force funeral planner mode. I had our speakers, mixer and microphones brought in so everyone could hear whoever was talking that wanted to share stories about Ben. There were so many people that got up and spoke and there was so much laughing going on, I wondered if the funeral director would think we were having a party instead of a funeral. The wake went on for close to three hours with people getting up to speak one after another.

Ben had touched the lives of all these people and everyone had great stories to tell. I think everyone in that room understood that Ben would not want us to be sad. To my husband, life was a party. Life was about God, family, friends, laughter and fun. I guess we probably should have had the gathering of friends at one of the karaoke venues downtown instead. He would have loved that.

The next day I went along with the funeral director in the hearse for the one-hour ride to take Ben's body to the crematory. He told me that he had witnessed many wakes in his time and Ben's was the best he had ever seen. I told him, "That's exactly the way Ben would have wanted it." It was raining that day, much like the night Ben died, and I just sat there looking out the window watching the rain come down as the flashbacks started and repeated in my mind all the way there. I had taken another pill that morning to help me hold myself together as I was now starting to deal with flashbacks more frequently, and I did not want to break down in front of anyone. We arrived and I placed a love letter I'd written to my husband the night before in his hand along with a picture and kissed him goodbye as I watched his body being placed inside the oven and watched as the button was pushed to start the process. It was a very long, sad, quiet ride back to Nashville, but I did what needed to be done despite the difficulty.

"You know what makes me sad? You do! Maybe we should chug on over to namby-pamby land, where maybe we can find some self-confidence for you, ya' Jack Wagon!"

– Geico Commercial, R. Lee Ermey

CHAPTER 4

Disarmament (Death by Human Resources)

THE NIGHT OF BEN'S DEATH, I HAD been informed that the Metro Nashville Police Department offers a Victim Intervention Program for victims of violent crime. This is a free counseling service to those Nashville residents affected by violent crime and is available as long as you need it. Even though I knew it was available, I kept talking myself out of it, because I have a degree in psychology and I thought I should be able to handle this on my own. I tried for a few months to deal with it. I did pretty well acting like everything was okay until one day I ended up crying non-stop in the middle of work and scaring the heck out of my already concerned co-workers at the college. I was dealing with anger, guilt, sadness, fear, depression and loneliness.

So I reluctantly made the decision to go get some counseling. I went for my first session in a large brick building in downtown Nashville that housed the counseling office. This building housed many different offices as well. The counseling office had a waiting room and the receptionist at her desk behind an open glass window. After checking in and waiting for a few minutes, I was taken back to a room where I met a counselor. (I will call her Irma.) I began to tell Irma of everything that happened to my husband and myself. It took me about 45 minutes to tell her everything after she started asking me questions.

I left that session feeling okay but not really feeling like this was going to make a significant difference. I had not discussed anything with her that I would not discuss with my best friends or family and I still did not see the real point in it but tried to keep an open mind. I just wanted the pain to go away and I thought "what the heck" it's free and I can use all the help I can get right now. I ended up going back for another session within the next week or two. Irma brought me back to her office and before long I was telling her how I had to leave my permitted gun locked in my vehicle the night Ben was killed.

She immediately looked at me and said, "Do you have a gun with you right now?" I said, "Well, of course I do. It's concealed in my purse. I am carrying legally and this building and your offices are not posted saying I can't." I reached into my purse to get my handgun carry permit out of my wallet so I could show her she had nothing to fear and that I am carrying legally. This woman totally flipped out on me and said, "Don't take your gun out! Don't take your gun out!" I just looked at her and said "Calm down, I am just getting my permit out to show you." Irma then looked at my permit and said, "You can't have that thing in here! You can never bring a gun in here! Our rules are no guns!"

I then told her that she has absolutely nothing to fear from me. I also told her that if that is their policy then they need to have a sign posted on the front door of the building clearly stating "no firearms allowed" so I will not be in an awkward position like I am right now. I also told her that if the building was posted then I would have never come inside. I just sat there in complete amazement at how she could behave like this after I poured my heart and soul out to her in my first session and was clearly no threat to her or anyone else. I am pretty sure this lady had to know I am a good and decent person that has just been through hell and has every reason in the world to carry a gun for self defense. I ended up leaving and I sent an email to her supervisor to let her know how disappointed I was that I am not welcome there because I carry a gun for my own self-defense and I do so with good reason.

I got a call from that supervisor and she was very nice but reiterated that they do not allow guns. She said, "Nikki, I had no idea it was really this bad for you, that you feel you have to carry a gun with you all the time." She informed me that they could call a security guard to walk me down to my car if it made me feel more comfortable after my sessions. I had never seen a security guard in or around that building the two times I had been there, so I wondered where this security guard was that she would call for me. She also told me that their office was safe because their office doors are locked.

I quickly informed her that if I was a bad guy (and I now have started to think like one) I would not bother with the locked door in the waiting room. If I wanted in, I would come straight on thru that open glass window at the receptionist desk. My intention was to open her eyes as to how vulnerable she and the others in the office really are. I told her that I would never harm an innocent person with my gun, but if someone came into that office to harm either myself or someone else, at least I would have the ability to try and stop them. She would not budge. I told her I would never be back. I hung up. I remember thinking how ridiculous that policy is.

Heck, I could have very easily lied when Irma asked if I had a gun and she would have never known otherwise. But that's what I get for being honest I suppose.

Yep, I was honest and not willing to disarm and now I have to pay for counseling that other victims like myself get for free. While I respect the Metro Nashville Police Department a great deal, I hope they will look into changing this policy. They should understand that there are many people coming into that office who have been brutalized and don't feel safe. If that person was stalked or is being stalked and they go through the steps to be legally armed, they should not be denied a service, which is provided for other victims simply because they choose to carry for their own self defense.

On their website it says their services are provided in an environment which supports cultural diversity with respect to: race, religion, creed and sexual orientation. But somehow it's okay to discriminate against me because I carry my legal handgun for self-defense. I then had to go seek out a psychologist on my own and this one would not be free. I would have to pay at least $30.00 an hour for counseling. I ended up finding a great psychologist who did not mind me carrying my gun at all. The first time I left my session, it was in the evening and pretty dark outside. He had offered to walk me to my car but then he stopped, thought about it and said "You're the one who should be walking me to my car!" with a big smile.

Dealing with Trauma

AT THE TIME, I WAS VERY SENSITIVE TO SUDDEN LOUD SOUNDS (anywhere but the shooting range). Some of the guys at the office would come by my door and slap their hand against the door just playing around while I was working. I am a pretty jovial, lighthearted person and love a good joke but this really bothered me. I about jumped out of my skin and finally had to tell them that it really was not funny and why. They are sweet guys and they simply did not think of it affecting me that way. These are the kind of guys that super glue a penny to the floor to watch people try and pick it up or leave a rubber rat in the hallway. They put toy spiders on fish line and drop them from the ceiling onto people for giggles. They are so much fun to be around and I loved working in the same building with them. It took me well over a year to overcome my sensitivity to sudden loud sounds.

I had already recognized I was dealing with PTSD (Post Traumatic Stress Disorder) because I clearly had the symptoms. As a psychology major, I can tell you that I studied this, and there is no way that someone can truly understand it until they have been through it themselves. I began to think like a bad guy and everywhere I would go, I would think of horrible scenarios of what might happen and how I could stop the bad guy before he killed innocent people. When I would walk down the street and pass a man standing there or a man sitting on a bench, I would wonder if that man aimed to harm me or others. Just about every man was a potential bad guy in my mind at this point. I now know what some of our soldiers deal with mentally as they come back home.

I knew if I shared too much with my psychologist about what I was dealing with mentally, he could diagnose me with PTSD and that could be used to revoke my permit and disarm me again. I was already scared enough as it was. I could not imagine having no real way to defend myself, so I kept much of my thoughts to myself. Which leads me to discuss Mental Illness and Gun Control.

Are there people who kill themselves after something this traumatic? Of course there are. There are also people like myself who pull through the grief, trauma and loss and are of no danger to themselves or anyone else. Should some-one who has been through something like this be disarmed? Absolutely not. Not unless they show signs of violence or very serious mental health issues. I believe it is normal after a traumatic event to have nightmares, day-mares and have some anxiety and depression. It's the person that has no emotions and does not deal with these temporary issues that I would be more concerned about. My anxiety would have only worsened if I did not have the ability to defend myself after what I had been through. I attended sessions for about four or five months until the psychologist said, "Nikki, I have seen many people that have gone through horrible things and I think you have come through faster than anyone I have ever seen."

At that point we made the decision that I no longer need-ed his services but I could always come back if I ever felt I needed to. There are still certain things that bother me and trigger my memories, but I have learned to just deal with it. It's just a new kind of normal for me. The bad moments are rare now, and I have figured out how to deal with those mo-ments should they pop up.

As I sit here writing this, that funny Geico commercial comes to mind with Marine Drill Sergeant "R. Lee Ermey" as the psychologist is yelling, "You know what makes me sad? You do! Maybe we should chug on over to namby-pamby land, where maybe we can find some self-confidence for you, ya' Jack Wagon!" I knew when I saw that commer-cial and I started laughing, that I was going to be okay. If someone has truly needed a psychologist and they can see the lighthearted humor in that commercial, I'd say they have made a pretty good start at recovery. I love R. Lee Ermey and that commercial still makes me smile. I had the pleasure of meeting him at the 2010 NRA Convention.

R. Lee Ermey and Nikki at the 2010 NRA Convention

Safe Commute and Guns on Campus

BEFORE BEN WAS MURDERED, WHEN I WAS HIRED ON AT THE college, their policy was that no firearms were allowed on the premises whatsoever. In order to be employed, I had to sign a form where I agreed not to bring a gun on the property or face being fired if they found one in a random vehicle search. If I wanted a job, I had to agree and sign the form. Normally, I would never do that, but I had been out of work for about eight months and I really needed this job. I remember thinking how incredibly stupid their policy was as a criminal or crazy person could easily come onto the property with a gun and get in the building with no resistance from anyone as the campus had no armed security and no security scanner locks. The college also had many windows that could easily be shot out and entered. The parking lot and the building is completely open to the public for access. All they were doing was preventing good folks from being able to protect themselves going to and from work. If I couldn't keep my legal, permitted firearm concealed and locked in my private vehicle, then I would be totally disarmed, and every place I stopped, going to and from work, such as the grocery store, pharmacy, gas station or walking back to my car in any of the parking lots associated with these places. Not everyone is lucky enough to live in and around posh communities with gates where they pull in their own driveway and feel fairly secure. I had to drive through some areas that are not so nice in order to get home. That red light or stop sign on the way home can end up being a great place for a carjacker to strike.

ع ع ع

MUCH TO MY DISMAY, I ENDED UP FINDING OUT THAT WHEN

they searched my stalker's truck the night of Ben's murder, they found two more guns (a shotgun and rifle), ammo, a baseball bat, binoculars, gloves, rope and a knife. It was at that point that I realized this man's intentions were most likely to not only kill Ben but to possibly kidnap me and kill me as well. Why else would he feel the need to have all those things in his truck? That certainly was no medical kit in his truck! Looking back now, it would have been very easy for my stalker to come to the college to kidnap me, harm me or kill me. I worked in two gun-free zones, the college and the restaurant. He chose the restaurant to attack. I have no idea if my stalker had ever followed me and knew where I worked during the day. My guess is that he most likely did know. I shutter to think what could have happened to the students and my co-workers if he had chosen the college. Everyone at the campus were sitting ducks and helpless to stop an attack from a deranged stalker. They would have most likely witnessed me being kidnapped or witnessed my death and who knows what else could have happened. When the bad guy is the only one with a gun, guess who wins?

You never know what you will do in a situation like that. My parents had always taught me as a child to never go with a bad guy even if he has a gun. I was taught he will most likely kill you anyway, and it is better to take your chances then and there rather than being kidnapped, brutally raped, tortured and then killed anyway. Although, had my stalker held the gun to a student's head and said "You either come with me or this person is going to die," I would have most likely said, "Yes Sir, I'm ready to go with you." These are the thoughts that went through my mind during this period of my life.

I have heard snide comments made about citizens who choose to carry. Common themes are "you are a vigilante" or "you just want to be a hero" or "you are paranoid." "Why would you go somewhere if you felt you needed a gun with you? Just stay home!" I have to ignore these kinds of comments and know that being prepared does not make me paranoid. People who have smoke detectors in their home are not called paranoid. People who have life insurance are not called paranoid. If you wear your seat belt does that make you paranoid? These people are simply being prepared.

Carrying a firearm for self defense is absolutely no different. I believe most people never really think something horrific will happen to them. I mean, after all, horrible things happen only to "other people" and I found myself thinking that very thing for many years before I took the steps to get my handgun carry permit. The truth of the matter is, bad things do happen to good people. Bad things can happen to good people in places that most of us would consider safe. Evil does not care if it is a nice neighborhood or a slum. Evil can come unexpectedly. It can pay a visit to you at anytime and anywhere. I learned that it can pay you a visit in the middle of a busy restaurant. The real question is whether you will be prepared to deal with that evil when it does come. Will you have the ability to defend yourself or will you end up being another statistic? What does society suggest a woman do if she has a stalker who could potentially be violent? Tell her to take out a restraining order that will most likely enrage the person who is stalking her and then expect this potentially violent person to respect that little piece of paper. Tell the woman she should just stay home, not work, not travel, not enjoy life and hunker down in her home and become a hermit? That kind of advice is re-victimizing someone who is already a victim.

Since losing my husband to a demented stalker, I have done my own research on what is being suggested out there on websites through organizations that are supposed to help victims of stalking. All the advice that is given basically tells the victim to change their entire life, don't go anywhere alone, change your phone number, don't have a routine, move, get a new job, tell people close to you about the stalker, take notes and keep track of what all the stalker does, take out a restraining order, etc. I have yet to see anything out there that tells a victim of stalking to consider getting the best defensive tool possible, a gun. No advice on steps to legally carry the gun in public to defend yourself against someone you fear may hurt you or kill you. No explanation of the basic human right of self-defense or how to legally act upon this if you find your life in imminent danger. Why is this subject made out to be such a taboo? I believe if this advice was given up front in a very factual and honest way, it would protect a great deal of good people.

The thought first crossed my mind about perhaps getting a carry permit when I heard the story of Channon Christian and Christopher Newsom of Knoxville, Tennessee. They were both brutally tortured and murdered after being kidnapped the night of Jan 7, 2007. They were carjacked in a parking lot while they were getting ready to leave a friend's apartment complex.

Chris was giving Channon a kiss when the armed attackers approached them that night. Chris and Channon were both in their early twenties and had their whole lives ahead of them – that is, until evil showed up unexpectedly, as it usually does. I had lived in the Knoxville area for many years and I knew of the area where these two young people were kidnapped. It was not what I considered a "bad area" and it was at this point I realized this sort of thing could happen to anyone. Channon and Chris just happened to be in the wrong place at the wrong time and they were defenseless. I won't get into all the gruesome details of everything these two young people went through before they were ultimately murdered as it is very disturbing. If you want to know more details you can look it up online yourself.

I can only imagine how many people made the decision to get their own carry permit after hearing this terrifying story. The story definitely moved me from carrying pepper spray to considering carrying a handgun.

ﻋ ﻋ ﻋ

I HAVE NOW MOVED ON TO WORK FOR THE TENNESSEE LEGISLA-ture as a staffer, where I am allowed to keep my gun locked in my vehicle in the legislative parking garage. While my pay did not go up, being able to have my gun in the car made all the difference in the world to me. I no longer have to fear losing my job for simply wishing to get home safe. However, I am not allowed to carry my legal gun within the Legislative Offices. We do have armed Tennessee State Troopers and Capitol Police in and around the building. Only Law Enforcement can carry in the Statehouse and Capitol. While we do have several Legislators who also happen to be Police Officers in their everyday regular lives and they are able to carry, it sure would be nice if my life meant just as much as theirs so that I too could have the ability to defend myself if need be.

These businesses that prevent law-abiding citizens from having their legal gun while at work should be held liable if anyone is ever harmed there by an armed perpetrator. Any criminal could just "walk right in" because the place is not truly secure. Also, I believe that if innocent people are harmed while trying to get home and not able to defend themselves because they were disarmed by a business, that business should be held liable. We in the gun rights community call this type of disarmament "Death by Human Resources."

What Might Happen

OFTEN WHEN DISCUSSING WHETHER PEOPLE SHOULD BE ABLE TO carry concealed handguns into restaurants that serve alcohol, I face hypothetical questions about what might go wrong. What if the permit holder gets drunk and goes out of control? What if the permit holder accidentally fires his gun and hits someone? Even with a horrible attack such as what happened to my husband and I, why would one believe that bringing another gun into the situation would make things better? Might not that permit holder shoot an innocent bystander instead of shooting the killer?

The debate over what might possibly go wrong isn't new. Every time gun control is debated it is the central theme of what gun control advocates worry about. When pilots tried to carry guns with them to protect their planes after the nine-eleven attacks, people quickly came up with a long list of what might go wrong. Just like claims against concealed carry permit holders, opponents were worried that pilots might get angry and recklessly fire their gun at others. Would they accidentally fire guns and cause planes to crash? I am not real sure why the anti-gunners are so concerned that a pilot may act reckless with a gun when they could simply act reckless with um ... a huge plane carrying a few hundred people! You have to wonder about some people and their process of reasoning.

What few Americans seem to know is that from the 1920s to 1963 the federal government required all commercial pilots flying with US mail to carry a gun and until 1979 pilots could choose whether or not they wanted to carry a gun. The rule was originally set up in case a plane with mail crashed and it was necessary for the pilot to protect the mail. Over all those decades there was never a fatal accident involving an armed airline pilot. Even without the screening or special psychological tests, there was never a problem reported. But despite all that history, it didn't stop gun-control advocates from opposing the carrying of guns by pilots to protect their passengers and themselves. Most commercial airline pilots for the major passenger airlines flew in the military where they were required to keep a loaded handgun with them whenever they flew outside the United States.

While it's conceivable that something going wrong *might* happen with concealed handguns in restaurants, these bad events are exceedingly unlikely. Just as with the pilots, no guesses about what might happen are necessary. According to OpenCarry.org, only a handful of states are left that do not allow citizens to carry in restaurants that serve alcohol. Of all the states that allow legal carry in restaurants that serve alcohol, none have repealed the law because of problems with permit holders. Some of these are open carry states, but the states with concealed carry laws keep extremely detailed information on the behavior of permit holders. In the first year of Virginia's Restaurant Carry Law, the number of major crimes involving firearms at bars and restaurants statewide declined 5.2%. There are over a quarter of a million right to carry permit holders in Virginia, but only 145 reported gun crimes occurred in Virginia bars and restaurants in 2010-2011 combined.

Take Florida, another state that allows carrying permitted concealed handguns in restaurants serving alcohol: Between October 1987 and December 31, 2010, Florida had issued permits to over 1.9 million people. But only 168 had their permits revoked for any firearms-related violations, and most of those involved people accidentally carrying their handguns into gun-free zones. But those 168 revocations represent a rate of just 0.009%. That is much less than one percent of permit holders. During the last 36 months from January 2008 to December 2010, the revocation rate was just

0.0003%. The analysis of the behavior of permit holders has been the same in state after state.

The claim is that more gun control will reduce crime, but there is a problem: every time that there has been a gun ban, murder and violent crime rates rose. Americans are familiar with how murder and violent crime rates rose in Washington, DC and Chicago after their gun bans. They may not have heard that their crime rates fell after the Supreme Court struck down their handgun bans and DC's gunlock laws. DC's murder rates have fallen by 36 percent since the June 2008 Heller decision, allowing DC residents to keep handguns in their home for self defense. Chicago's murder rate had fallen by 14 percent in the last six months of 2010 after the Supreme Court's McDonald decision compared to the last six months of 2009.

Unfortunately, banning guns over a smaller area, such as a restaurant, isn't any more successful, and the problem is the same in both cases. Law-abiding citizens are more likely to obey the ban, whereas criminals are more likely to disobey it. When this happens things can go very wrong. Instead of making things safer for victims, we unintentionally make them safer for criminals. Criminals have less to worry about in attacking victims.

Take a simple example. Suppose that you or your family were being seriously threatened by a stalker. Would you feel safer putting a sign on your house saying that your house is a "gun-free zone?" Probably not. But that is in fact what we do on all sorts of places such as restaurants and schools. Why do we put signs up on those places when we wouldn't dare think about putting them up on our homes?

Ironically, Americans seem to think they are unique about multiple-victim shootings. But in fact, these horrible attacks are about as common in Europe despite their much stricter gun-control laws. Few seem to know that Germany has had the two worst K-12 public school shootings, and both of those have taken place during the last decade since gun bans have been put in place.

Obviously, there are great cultural differences between countries. So any comparison we make will be less than perfect. But statistical works have attempted to account for the variable factors and have looked at the changes in attack rates before and after the passage of right-to-carry laws.

Let's look at a few of the cases in Europe over the last decade.

- Zug, Switzerland, September 27, 2001: A man murdered 15 members of a cantonal parliament.

- Tours, France, October 29, 2001: Four people were killed and ten wounded when a French railway worker started killing people at a busy intersection in the city.

- Nanterre, France, March 27, 2002: A man killed eight city councilors after a city council meeting.

- Erfurt, Germany, April 26, 2002: A former student killed 18 people at a secondary school.

- Freising, Germany, February 19, 2002: Three people killed and one wounded.

- Turin, Italy, October 15, 2002: Seven people were killed on a hillside overlooking the city.

- Madrid, Spain, October 1, 2006: A man killed two employees and wounded another at a company that he was fired from.

- Emsdetten, Germany, November 20, 2006: A former student murdered 11 people at a high school.

- Southern Finland, November 7, 2007: Seven students and the principal were killed at a high school.

- Naples, Italy, September 18, 2008: Seven dead and two seriously wounded in a public meeting hall.

- Kauhajoki, Finland, September 23, 2008: Ten people were shot to death at a college.

- Winnenden, Germany, March 11, 2009: A 17-year-old former student killed 15 people, including nine students and three teachers.

- Lyon, France, March 19, 2009: Ten people injured after a man opened fire on a nursery school.

- Athens, Greece, April 10, 2009: Three people killed and two people injured by a student at a vocational college.

- Vienna, Austria, May 24, 2009: One dead and 16 wounded in an attack on a Sikh Temple.

- Espoo, Finland, December 31, 2009: Four killed while shopping at a mall on New Year's Eve.

- Cumbria, England, June 2, 2010: Twelve people killed by a British taxi driver.

The key point is that gun-free zones didn't stop these killers from committing their crimes. We don't have to guess how permit holders behave. America has seen many cases where permit holders have stopped multiple-victim public shootings, and they have stopped these attacks without shooting any innocent bystanders or getting themselves shot by police. Hysterical discussions about what *might* go wrong do not make sense when we have decades of experience with these laws all across the United States.

I will never forget Suzanna Hupp telling me "Nikki, don't be afraid to stand up for what you believe in. You will be amazed at the impact you can have on other's lives."

CHAPTER 5

Fighting for Legislation

I**N THE DAYS AND WEEKS AFTER BEN'S** death, I was on my computer constantly. I sent emails to every legislator in the Tennessee General Assembly about my husband's murder and being denied the right of self defense.

I knew there were some very strong Second Amendment supporters in the legislature, who were already pushing a bill to allow concealed carry in restaurants, and it was my goal to reach them. In my research I found out that the senator who sponsored the Restaurant Carry Bill was a democrat by the name of Doug Jackson. I thought to myself, *democrat? A democrat actually sponsored this bill? You have got to be kidding me?* I had thought that it was the democrats that wanted to take guns away from law-abiding people. Boy was I ever wrong!

Here in Tennessee, unlike some states, we have more than several solid Second Amendment supporters on the democrat side in our state house. These legislators realize it is NOT just about duck hunting or having a gun only in your home. It is about being able to defend yourself anywhere you have a right to be. It is a basic human right.

The republicans were the ones that mostly carried the Restaurant Carry Bill through, but I was surprised and excited by the democrat support and realized this is not a partisan issue. So, I found Senator Jackson's phone number and I made the call while still in my pajamas outside, sitting on the hood of Ben's old pickup truck.

The senator had remembered seeing the story of Ben's shooting on the news, but what he didn't know was that I was a permit holder and my gun was locked in my vehicle that night because of the law. Our story was exactly what Senator Jackson needed to show the importance of the bill. Senator Jackson told me that he might need me at some point soon to help get the bill passed.

A Friend in Suzanna Hupp

OVER THE NEXT SEVERAL DAYS, I DECIDED THAT I NEEDED TO contact the one person who had been on my mind since the night Ben was killed. That person was Suzanna Hupp (Survivor of Luby's Cafeteria Massacre in Killeen, Texas). What happened to Ben and I was similar to what happened to Suzanna and her parents back in 1991 in a Luby's restaurant.

I had learned of Suzanna in my handgun carry permit class, and I was mortified when I watched her testifying about how a madman shot and killed 23 people, including her parents, and wounded 20 others in the cafeteria. Suzanna had left her gun locked in her car because of Texas State Law and felt that, if not for the law, she could have possibly stopped the gunman before he took so many lives.

I was already a member of (SAS) the Second Amendment

Sisters organization, and I decided to reach out to my friend Barbara, who is the Director of the Tennessee SAS to see if she knew of any way for me to contact Suzanna Hupp. It turned out that Suzanna was on the Board of Directors for this organization, and Barbara and I made my story known to the senior members. Those senior members ended up giving me Suzanna's cell phone number, and that is when I made the phone call I will never forget.

I dialed Suzanna's number. I told my story as quickly as I could, all the while thinking to myself, *this is a very busy woman.* She has been speaking on this for many years and she was a legislator in Texas and probably won't have the time to talk to me (a perfect stranger.)

We talked a good 30 minutes. I will never forget Suzanna telling me, "Nikki, don't be afraid to stand up for what you believe in. You will be amazed at the impact you can have on other's lives." She told me, "You know Nikki, I'm mad that my father couldn't be here to teach his grandchildren to play golf. My dad was an excellent golfer and he would have loved to know my children. My children have been robbed of knowing their grandparents and that really upsets me." She gave me some tips on what to expect from the media and talked to me about what she went through in the aftermath of her tragedy. After that very poignant conversation, I got to work.

Before my husband's death, I was like most people when it came to my convictions. If I believed in something I would say so if it ever came up in conversation, I would answer a poll here and there when they would come up, but I never really got involved in any mass movement for change. Unfortunately, it was not until I lost Ben that I realized how important getting involved and speaking up really is. I hope as you read this book, you realize how important it is for you to be personally involved to ensure your rights are upheld. Do not wait until something tragic happens before you decide to do something about it. It is important to use your civil authority for change you see as necessary.

I started joining gun forums online and found the Tennessee Firearms Association and went to my first meeting. I joined the Tennessee Gun Owners Association and talked to everyone I could. I was starting to meet some wonderful people in the Second Amendment rights community, and they were all very supportive. These people helped pull me through a very difficult time in those first months as a widow.

I believe in responsible gun ownership by law-abiding citizens, knowing the law and following safety rules. With that said, I realized that publicly standing up for something such as "Restaurant Carry" which was viewed as such a divisive issue by some, was not going to make me "well liked" by certain people. I understood the concerns of citizens who fear guns and alcohol "mixing." That is something I have NEVER condoned. Anytime you speak out publicly in support or against something, you will always manage to tick off some segment of the population. I would be labeled by many as crazy, a gun-nut, right-wing extremist, paranoid and I was even called by one blogger "murderer." While human beings have a huge capacity for kindness and love, they also can be very cruel. It really hurt to have someone (who did not even know me but knew what happened to me) call me a murderer. Needless to say, I had to develop some thick skin rather quickly.

Nikki was honored to meet Suzanna Hupp while on the
set of *Fox Business* with John Stossel.

Day on the Tennessee State Floor

I GOT A CALL AT 6:00 AM AND ON THE OTHER LINE WAS SENATOR Jackson saying, "Nikki, how would you like to be my guest here at the Tennessee State Capitol today as I share your story with everyone on the floor as we vote to override Governor Phil Bredesen's veto of the Restaurant Carry Bill?" I told him, "Senator, I will be there. I'm getting ready right now!" I had never been to the Capitol before and I was very nervous. I had no idea what to expect.

As I was getting ready, I remembered how I had sat in Ben's office all alone on April 6, 2009 (just four days after Ben's death) and listened to former Speaker of the Tennessee House "Jimmy Naifeh" argue against the Restaurant Carry Bill via live stream video on my computer. His words on the house floor were, "Here we are doing this at this time where just last week, in a restaurant in Nashville, someone was shot and killed."

In all fairness, Representative Naifeh had no idea at the time he made that statement, that the murder he was referring to was of a man whose wife was a permit holder that had to leave her gun locked in her car that night and was denied her right to protect him because of votes that Jimmy made himself. The fact that he used our tragedy against the bill that I supported made me cringe. It also upset me that he fought against this kind of legislation for 15 years and kept it from being voted on by stacking committees where this kind of legislation would ultimately die every time.

I was stunned how a man that is a member of the NRA and a permit holder himself could not see how the current law left people helpless, ready to be picked off by those who could care less about his "laws." Had the Restaurant Carry

Nik,

I love you so much, and even though I've been laid off I feel like it's going to be okay because we have such a wonderful marriage and we think so much alike that I know together we will work hard and always put each other first so we will always have happiness.

To me, loving you is a pleasure. I look forward to seeing you smile. I love when the phone rings and it is you. I love waking up with you. I just love being with you. Like the card said, "Life doesn't get any better than this," and it's true. My life is so much better because you are in it and I love that. I appreciate that and I value that more than anything else.

I love you, Nik.

Ben

Above is the text of Ben's final love letter to Nikki.

Law been in place the night my stalker showed up at Jonny's (instead of being fought over for almost 15 years) perhaps Ben would have had a chance to live.

I will never know if I could have saved Ben because I was denied that chance. I actually know Representative Naifeh now, and he is a pretty nice man from what I can tell. I have passed him in the hallway at the legislature and he will nod and say hello, I do the same also. I have gotten past my anger and had to learn to forgive, but never will I ever forget. Needless to say, I was ready and willing to shoot down (pun intended) what he had said on the House floor by having my story told in the Senate.

The Senator's Assistant was waiting on me outside the Capitol and walked me into the Senate Chamber where I sat next to Senator Jackson. The media was there and the cameras were everywhere. I gave Senator Jackson the last love letter that my husband had written to me before his death to be read on the floor. Ben wrote it just three weeks before his passing, and I knew that perhaps that love letter might spring some life to this vote getting ready to take place.

I wanted these lawmakers to feel my sense of loss and know the heart and spirit of my late husband. Senator Jackson did an incredible job of relaying my story to everyone in the Senate Chamber. The senator reminded everyone that the Restaurant Carry Bill specifically states that you must be at least 21 years of age, pass a background check, have your fingerprints taken, complete the state permit training, and you cannot be under the influence of drugs or alcohol while carrying. Senator Jackson read letters from law enforcement personnel who were supporting the bill.

That was important, because our governor at the time, Phil Bredesen, lead the public to believe that law enforcement did not support the bill. I believe the governor even pulled a "Slick Willy" to show the public law enforcement's strong stand against this bill. There was a large group of police chiefs attending a convention down the street from the Capitol and they were supposedly asked to come over and meet the governor during a break. One of our legislators was informed (by someone involved but unwilling to come forward publicly) that it was then and only then that these officers were told about what the governor intended to do (use them as his personal backdrop for his veto signing ceremony).

Now I don't know about you but, if I was a police officer and I was invited over to the Capitol to meet the governor and obviously expected to be his "backdrop," wouldn't it make me look bad if I refused to do it? Would you want to openly contradict the governor? Granted, most of these officers were police chiefs and, sometimes, when you get up to that rank of law enforcement, you become politically influenced. Most rank and file officers support this kind of legislation and understand that the citizenry has a right to defend themselves wherever they have a right to be. They see firsthand the fact that bad guys don't follow the law. The officers I have spoken to would much rather find an innocent person with a smoking gun and a dead bad guy than the other way around. Unfortunately, these officers fear coming forward and speaking up because it could put their job in jeopardy due to retaliation from those higher up. I find that pretty sad.

Senator Jackson talked about how back in 1996 when shall-issue permits were allowed in our state, the media went nuts with stories of how our state would be a blood bath and our society would mimic the days of the Wild West. People feared that permit holders would be shooting each other at the supermarket over a loaf of bread. Well, that blood bath by permit holders never happened. There were no shootouts over SunBeam or Wonder Bread. Amazingly, none of those media outlets have done stories on how very WRONG they were after all. I have yet to see a news report on violent crime numbers before the law went in place and those numbers now that the law has been in place for many years. After the senator's speech, I was recognized on the floor, the votes were taken, and the Restaurant Carry Bill that had been vetoed by Governor Bredesen was overridden and passed by a vote of 21 to 9.

Nikki and Senator Jackson on the Tennessee state floor.

On November 20, 2009 I sat in Chancellor Bonnyman's courtroom in Davidson County Tennessee as the Restaurant Carry Law (that had now been in place for four months with no shootouts) was being challenged for being unconstitutionally vague. A group of restaurant owners in the very liberal part of Nashville, hired a team of slick attorneys to try and have the new law overturned. These restaurant owners didn't like the new law and were hell bent on getting it overturned.

One of the restaurant owners who was always in front of a camera talking about the foolishness of the new law was a man by the name of "Richard." Richard saw fit to yell at me in the courthouse when I tried calmly speaking with him about the importance of the law. One thing I have learned is, there are just certain people who cannot have a healthy, calm debate without a blood vessel popping out of their head and steam coming out of their ears. I can understand why Richard does not like this law, as I feel his temper may cause him not to trust himself if he were armed in public. It became apparent to me that Richard was most likely projecting his own "Ticking Time Bomb" personality onto others. I'm fine with Richard not carrying.

At first, the restaurant owners were kicking and screaming about it not being safe for employees and patrons. When they figured out that argument really would not work after OSHA released their statement that is was not a safety hazard, they then decided to come from an angle of being concerned for permit holders. How thoughtful of them right?!

The bill said you could carry a permitted handgun in any restaurant that serves alcohol but they must serve one meal a day, five days a week, with an adequate kitchen and staff. The argument was made that a permit holder would not be able to properly discern this simply by looking at an establishment from the street and walking in. If they walked in and the restaurant did not fall within these guidelines, the permit holder would be breaking the law without even knowing it.

The group of restaurant owners filing the lawsuit got a group of people they knew who had permits (who remained anonymous of course) to state they were afraid they might break the law because the new law was just too vague.

The law was overturned that day in court and deemed unconstitutionally vague. This day was what would have been my husband's 50th birthday. I thought about Ben through the whole trial. I was pretty down after the verdict as myself and many others had fought hard for the passage of that law. It was back to the drawing board for our legislators. The bill was re-drafted to remove any vagueness and boy did they ever remove it.

The new bill opened up permitted carry TO ANY establishment that serves alcohol. Period. It ended up passing and the law was back in place by July 2010. I chuckled as I thought how those restaurant owners just shot themselves in the foot by taking the first bill to court. Richard, bless his soul, can still post his little "no guns allowed" sign and have a false sense of security in his restaurant but any restaurant owner who wants legally armed patrons in their establishment are now free to do so. There still have been no shootouts by permit holders in any restaurants or bars since the law was put in place. The hypotheticals they kept harping about have never come true.

ﻉ ﻉ ﻉ

In November 2009, I would spend even more time at the Capitol: This is when I started working as a Legislative Assistant for the Tennessee House of Representatives. Every day driving to the Capitol, I would pass by the prison that my husband's murderer sat in while awaiting his fair trial. Every day I would think, "You fool, look at what you have done to yourself."

I'll never forget my first day working for the legislature. I was so excited and it was an honor to be a part of the process of seeing that great laws are passed and helping the citizens of Tennessee.

I stayed late one day in my new office trying to organize my files and learn as much as I could on my own from reading information online and in the notes I received from other staffers who had been there many years. I decided to take a stroll up to the Capitol building that night all alone. I walked onto the State House Floor and thought, Holy cow, I actually work here! I walked out on the balcony overlooking the city of Nashville and again thought, I can't believe I actually work here! Then I made my way to the Senate Floor where I had been a guest of Senator Jackson earlier in the year. I never dreamed that life would bring me here.

What I found really odd was the first time I saw legislators give each other hell on the floor and then see them out having dinner together later. They will rip each other apart out on the floor sometimes and you'd swear they can't stand each other, but somehow most of them are able to remain friends and move on until the next giant debate.

I too have learned that you can be firm on your stance for a piece of legislation and you can think that the guy who doesn't see it your way has a few screws loose, but at the end of the day you still treat them as a human being. That was a hard pill for me to swallow when I first got to the State House. I would end up in the elevator with some of these legislators that have been against the bill that could have saved my husband's life had it been passed long ago. I eventually had to let go of my anger and realize that sometimes there are people you just can't influence, because they have never been there themselves. You just pray they never have to endure the same kind of pain you went through.

I have a plaque hanging in my office that I look at every-day that says, "Put your big girl panties on and deal with it!" I also have a sign up that says, "Often the greatest growth takes place under the hardest of circumstances. Look deeply to learn the lessons of the coldest, most painful times, for within them lies your greatest potential for transformation." With each frustration that came my way, I would read these sayings to stay grounded.

One thing that was scary for me when I started work-ing for the legislature was the parking situation I was in. Because I was new, I did not have Legislative Plaza parking privileges just yet. So I could not park at the State House Legislative garage until a spot came open when an employee left. This took several months. I had to park down the hill off Charlotte Ave. in a parking garage next to the bus station. Many times I would get off from work and it would be dark and I would have to walk down past that bus station to get to my car. There were always sketchy looking people that hung out on the streets down there at night. Hoods over their heads, loitering around in dark corners, staring at you and taunting you as you walked by.

As I have said before, the Tennessee legislature does not allow staffers and legislators who have a permit (anyone other than law enforcement), to carry while within the leg-islative offices. So I was disarmed walking alone to my car in the evening, which was quite unsettling. After what I had been through, this was extremely hard for me. I feared being mugged and assaulted or maybe even worse while walking to that garage. I often thought to myself, if I get killed tonight on the way to my car, then and only then will the legislature pass a bill to allow permit holders to carry within their legis-lative walls. I really did not want to be the test case for that.

I had to wait like everyone else who was new to eventually work my way up the parking spot list. I hardly knew anyone at this time, but I tried to hitch a ride down to the garage with the one or two people I did know. However, sometimes they were not available. A few times I even paid a taxi to take me down to the garage and directly to my car. I wondered how many other new staffers felt as concerned as I was about making that walk. Finally, my parking spot eventually came, and I didn't have to walk down that scary street any longer.

Self-defense is a basic human right, and, any lawmaker who does not believe that, should be voted out of office and never be allowed to return. It is our duty as a citizenry of the United States to make sure our rights are protected. I would encourage people to not just look at these legislative candidates party affiliation when deciding if they are pro-Second Amendment, but do the research to see where they really stand on your rights.

I have seen republicans who vote against self-defense bills just like I have seen democrats who support them. I have seen republicans who support self-defense legislation and have witnessed democrats shoot these bills down as well. Our Second Amendment is not a partisan issue, it is a civil rights issue. Just because their campaign website says they support the Second Amendment does not mean they really do. You need to dig in and see where the candidates stand before you cast your vote. Ask them specific questions on where they believe you have a right to defend yourself and don't let them dance around the question.

Fighting for Second Amendment Rights in Ohio

I'VE ALSO PUSHED FOR STATES BESIDES TENNESSEE TO CHANGE their gun laws. I got to know the "Ohioans for Concealed Carry" and the "Buckeye Firearms Association" through online forums and phone conversations. These two grass-roots organizations were a wonderful outlet for me, and I am honored to call them friends. The people in Second Amendment organizations across the country are the backbone of what makes America great.

These are people who understand our Constitution and what our founding fathers meant when they wrote, "A well regulated Militia, being necessary to the security of a free state, the right of the people to keep and bear arms shall not be infringed." Many of these people have been through close calls or actually been victims themselves or simply do not ever want to be a victim after hearing stories like my own. You would also be surprised how many of them are ex-military or law enforcement and almost all are NRA Members.

I was asked by "Ohioans for Concealed Carry" to come testify before the Ohio legislature in favor of their own Restaurant Carry Bill. They put me on a plane bound for the Capitol in Columbus, Ohio. I had always been terrified of flying and was not thrilled about getting on a plane. I had never testified before a legislature and was quite nervous. I stood before the Public Safety and Homeland Security Committee and told my story, hoping that somehow those Legislators would see how disarming law-abiding citizens creates victims.

I tried my best to not break down while giving my speech, but I eventually succumbed to my emotions at the tail end for a brief moment. Committee Chairwoman Linda Bolon (D) told me that it was the most compelling testimony she had ever heard. The sponsor of the bill in the House, (Representative Danny Bubp-R) asked everyone in the committee room who was in favor of the bill to come into the "Washington Room" afterwards.

Here Representative Bubp spoke of the importance of the

bill being demonstrated through my experience as he held my hand and looked at me with tears in his eyes and explained that in his own way, he understood my sense of loss. He had seen our soldiers die while serving as a colonel in the Marine Corps in Iraq. These men and women fighting for our "rights" and the sacrifices they make is something I will never forget and will never take for granted. Freedom is not free. It spoke volumes to me that a Colonel in the Marine Corps was the sponsor of this bill. A few months later, I was asked to return to Ohio and testify before the Senate. Suzanna Hupp and I both testified this time around.

The Ohio legislature ended up passing the Restaurant Carry Bill and on June 30 2011, Governor John Kasich signed the bill into law. As another odd coincidence, June 30 was the day that I first met my husband back in 2007. I was invited by the governor to attend the signing ceremony and had the honor of dotting the "i" in his last name on the bill. It was a pretty incredible moment for me knowing that I helped shape a law that may very well save some innocent person's life someday by giving them a fighting chance at survival. Something Ben and I were denied.

Signing of the Ohio Restaurant Carry Bill with Governor Kasich

Speaking for Second Amendment Rights in Arkansas

I WAS BEING FLOWN IN TO LITTLE ROCK, ARKANSAS TO SHARE my story for the "Second Amendment March" Rally. I had met the Carlton family through my advocacy work and they invited me into their home to stay while I was in Little Rock as a guest speaker. It touched me that this family who really did not know me (only knew my story), welcomed me into their home. That is one great thing about people within the Second Amendment/gun-rights community: we support one another and we trust one another. We are not the nut jobs the media tries to paint us as.

The Carltons are pharmacists and own their own pharmacy. They are both armed every day they work. They have seen all the addicts and pill seekers, and know that there is a strong possibility that someone may try to rob their business or maybe worse. They have seen the horror stories unfold on the news of pharmacists and others, who complied with the gunman 100 percent, only to be murdered by some addict looking for a quick fix with no regard for innocent lives.

I spoke in Little Rock, Arkansas at Barton Coliseum (which is a venue meant to hold about ten thousand people). I was thinking I would be speaking to several thousand people at this facility. Several legislators, gubernatorial candidates and activists like Skip Coryell (founder of the Second Amendment March) and myself were scheduled to speak.

Once there, we were disappointed to see only about two hundred people that had attended. For me, it was a great learning experience in getting myself prepared mentally to speak. While I was disappointed in the turnout, it was not a problem for me, because I knew the media would be there. If my story made it on camera, then my message would reach the intended thousands. Sure enough, the cameras were there and the thousands were reached when it aired that night.

After the rally, I went to eat with several permit holders and was surprised to learn that in the state of Arkansas, you can actually have a drink or two (as long as you are not intoxicated) and carry your permitted gun. As long as you are under the .08 blood alcohol content limit and can drive your vehicle, you can carry your legal gun. I had no idea. We had gone into a Mexican restaurant for dinner and I was shocked when the armed people at my table were ordering a margarita.

I looked at them and said, "What are you doing?! You're gonna get us thrown in jail!" They all smiled and told me "Honey, you're in Arkansas." The law has not been repealed in Arkansas which tells me that permit holders are acting responsibly even when allowed to drink within moderation while carrying. No big surprise there. I guess I can understand the reasoning behind their law. If you are able to legally drive a vehicle that is essentially one large bullet capable of killing many, then you should also be able to carry your legal firearm. I don't recommend drinking and carrying but I certainly see no major issues coming from those who lawfully carry in Arkansas. I look at it this way, the people who were in Jonny's Sports Bar that were three sheets to the wind the night the shooting happened and ran out of the restaurant, got in their cars and drove, put more people at risk than these permit holders ever could.

On to Kentucky

THE SECOND AMENDMENT MARCH WAS WORKING ITS WAY TO my birth state, Kentucky. I was born in Owensboro, Kentucky and lived there until my father moved our family to Tennessee when I turned ten. I was asked to come speak at the Capitol. The Bartley family who were organizers of the event took me in. This was another great family who opened their home to a complete stranger so she would have a place to lay her head at night. This was better than any hotel, they had guns and I knew I was safe! The rally was held on the grounds of the Capitol in Frankfort.

As I started my speech I looked out over the crowd and said, "How does it feel to be in the safest place in Kentucky?!" I personally have never felt so safe in my entire life. Over 500 people legally armed – and guess what? Nobody was killed. Not a single shot fired. Yet the anti-gun people would have you believe that there should have been blood all over the Kentucky State House lawn.

After my speech on the State House steps, I was asked for an interview by one of the local media crews that was there. The reporter who was getting ready to interview me started telling me of her own ordeal. This was a young woman that was probably about 23 years old, long blonde hair, blue eyes and beautiful. She heard my story and told me that she was now going to go get her own handgun carry permit.

She told me that she was being stalked and she was some-what scared and especially now after hearing what happened to Ben and I. She had already discussed it with her father and he agreed she needed to be armed. It did not surprise me that she had a stalker. Many women (especially attractive ones) on TV do tend to get the unwanted attention of a number of weirdo types.

US Senate candidate Rand Paul and Nikki in Kentucky at
the Second Amendment March State Rally

The media gave that worthless waste of flesh exactly what he wanted when he mailed them his videos just before he went on his murderous rampage. He wanted to be remembered, and the media did his bidding! I wish the media would stop giving these animals the attention they want.

CHAPTER 6

The BBC

IT WAS NOT LONG AFTER THE Restaurant Carry Bill passed in Tennessee that the BBC (British Broadcasting Corporation) contacted me. They heard of my story and wanted to interview me at a shooting range. I thought, *Oh Geez, here we go. They are going to make me out to be some kind of Annie Oakley wanna-be.* I really did not want to be filmed shooting my gun because of this very concern.

I just wanted to speak with them, but they wanted my gun on film. I thought about what all they could do in the editing room to make me look bad, but came to the realization that they are going to do whatever they are going to do and I just have to be myself and talk about the facts.

When they came to Nashville for the interview I just kept thinking to myself: *Dear God, thousands of people are going to see this and I have got to shoot well under pressure.* I chose to shoot my Ruger SP-101 .357 Magnum. I shot within the triangle "center mass," which was not a big deal because it was close range, self-defense shots.

Nikki Goeser, seen here in her Tennessee Firearms Association shirt, at the firing range with the BBC.

I had good reason to be nervous about talking with British reporters.

The British cannot own or carry handguns for self-defense. In 1997 the UK Government imposed a nationwide ban on the purchasing and ownership of all handguns following the massacre in Dunblane, Scotland. On March 13, 1996 a legal gun owner that I will call "TH" (because he is a monster and does not deserve to be remembered) gained entry into Dunblane Primary School's gymnasium and opened fire on five- and six-year-old children, killing 16 children along with their teacher who was trying to shield them before "TH" killed himself.

The families and friends of the victims lobbied to have all guns banned and they got what they asked for. Crime in the UK has now skyrocketed since their passage of strict gun-control laws. Law-abiding people have no real means to defend themselves against a bad guy with a gun in the UK, but criminals simply ignore gun-control laws. When you outlaw guns, only outlaws will have guns.

German Television

AFTER THE BBC INTERVIEW AIRED, GERMAN TELEVISION contacted me. I was already scheduled to speak at Barrett Firearms along with Senator Jackson for a Second Amendment rally and they wanted to come out and get my story that day. In my mind I could see the all-too-familiar film footage of Nazi soldiers loading up innocent people who they regarded as political dissidents and transporting them away for extermination. I could see women and children separated from their husbands and then children taken away to be sent to Dr. Josef Mengele to be experimented on and tortured before being killed themselves. This is the cruel reality of what can happen when citizens don't have the means to fight back against a tyrannical government.

Here in the United States we have become spoiled in our freedom to the point that many Americans forget how important the freedom to keep and bear arms really is. I see it every day in the news where people have become indifferent to their rights and just allow them to be slowly taken away.

When the German news crew got there and started speaking with me, I could tell they did not approve of gun ownership and it was lingering in every question they asked me. I would imagine if you could sit down and speak to any of the millions of people who died at the hands of the cruel Nazi SS, they would probably tell you that they would have much rather had a fighting chance at survival instead of being easy victims.

When the Nazis invaded Poland and forced over three hundred thousand innocent Jews into the Warsaw Ghetto, resistance fighters held off the Nazis for 28 days. The only reason they were able to fight is because guns, ammo and grenades were being smuggled in. Eventually they were overtaken because they were outgunned. If gun control had not been put in place before Hitler took control and continued by Hitler, I believe history may have been very different.

The Media Glorifies Murderers

WHY DO WE HEAR SO MUCH IN THE MEDIA ABOUT MURDERERS instead of the victims and their loved ones who are left behind to pick up the pieces? I can tell you the names of the two scumbags at Columbine High School who murdered their classmates and teachers, but for some reason the names of the victims do not come to mind. Why? Because these two murderer's faces and names were paraded across national television for weeks and months, and still are on occasion to this day.

This kind of glorification gives every sicko out there ideas of how they too can become famous. I can tell you the name of the murderer at Virginia Tech, and I can even picture him in my mind because it was pretty much branded there by all the pictures and video of him that the media spewed everywhere.

The media gave that worthless waste of flesh exactly what he wanted when he mailed them his videos just before he went on his murderous rampage. He wanted to be remembered, and the media did his bidding! I wish the media would stop giving these animals the attention they want. You probably notice I don't use Ben's murderer's name in my book. It is for this very reason. He does not deserve to be remembered as he is nothing more than a coward.

In multiple victim public shootings like Columbine High School and Virginia Tech, 75 percent of the time the killers themselves die at the scene. In many of the remaining 25 percent of the cases the killers just couldn't bring themselves to commit suicide. What is clear though is that these attacks were essentially attempts by these killers to commit suicide. But they wanted to commit suicide in a particular way, one that would garner them as much publicity and attention as possible, to go out with a bang.

This poses a real problem for law-enforcement. While police are extremely important in crime control (probably the most important single factor) police face several real problems in stopping attacks. The first is the issue of deterrence. Police catch criminals after they have committed a crime. In the case of multiple-victim public shootings where the criminal believes that he will die at the scene, the threat of police catching him after the fact is simply irrelevant.

Police are also at a strategic disadvantage. Take Israel as an example. For decades, while under terrorist attacks, Israel kept trying to put more police and military on the street. But if a terrorist was waiting on a bus with police or soldiers present, he has two options: either wait for the police to leave the bus before he attacks or kill the police first. Eventually Israel learned that they just didn't have enough money to hire enough police or soldiers to cover all the potential targets that terrorists might hit.

What Israel turned to in the early 1970s was to let citizens carry concealed handguns. About 15 percent of Israel's Jews are allowed to carry guns, and when the terror threat level increases, the national police chief will call on Israelis to make sure that they have a gun with them as they go about their business.

What seems to limit the carnage from these attacks is how quickly someone with a gun is able to arrive on the scene to stop the attack. This is extremely important. If these killers are committing their attack to generate news coverage, but someone is able to be there very quickly to stop the attack before many people are killed or injured, it takes away the warped benefit that the killer perceives he is getting from the crime. So the benefits of concealed handguns, include not only limiting the harm done when attacks occur by quickly getting someone there to stop the attack, but also the damage is reduced because the potential killers are deterred from making an attack to begin with.

The Research Is Conclusive

RESEARCH BY JOHN LOTT AND BILL LANDES EXAMINED ALL the multiple-victim public shootings from 1977 to 1999 and found that states with right-to-carry laws saw that multiple-victim public shootings declined by 60 percent. To the extent that these attacks still occur, they take place where permitted concealed handguns are not allowed.

The mass shooting in an Aurora, Colorado movie theater that left 12 people dead and 59 injured made headlines in 2012 and a call for gun bans and more gun-free zones. The shooter was considered a brilliant science student in a graduate program, never been diagnosed as mentally ill and did not have a criminal record at all. Therefore, he was able to purchase his guns legally. After the shooting, people came forward to say how odd he was and spoke of red-flag-type behavior that was simply overlooked.

What many may not realize is that within a 20-minute radius around the shooter's bomb-laced, booby-trapped apartment were movie theaters that allowed handgun permit holders to carry there. Out of all of these movie theaters, only one was posted "no guns allowed," and that is the theater where the shooter chose to carry out a mass murder. It was not the closest theater nor was it the most populated theater. Had he chosen any of the other theaters, handgun carry permit holders most likely would have been in the theater and he most likely would not have been able to pull off such a grand murderous rampage. He chose a place where he knew he would be met with no resistance from those he intended to kill.

People have argued that these places need metal detectors but in this case the killer came in through a side emergency door. A metal detector at the front entrance would have done nothing. However, armed law-abiding citizens inside the theater could have done something to prevent the carnage. Even with all the protective gear the shooter had on, being hit with multiple rounds in a vest can knock a predator down, slow him down and create a situation where he can be stopped. A potential killer knowing their victims may be armed can also deter them from engaging in the first place.

A Vanderbilt Law Professor, who had developed a website called gunfreediningtn.org, once told me that I overestimate the intelligence of criminals. He developed this website as a reference for Tennessee residents who wish to dine in restaurants that are posted "no guns allowed" in peace where they can feel safe. He even has a street team that goes out to restaurants and tries to get them to put up "no guns allowed" signs. They even provide the signs! I was on the news beside him as he announced his new website so I could give the opposite viewpoint on the issue. I tried to explain that this would not only be a reference tool for customers but also for anyone looking to make an easy robbery hit or worse. I think this law professor underestimates the intelligence of criminals. Obviously the Aurora movie theater shooter knew exactly what he was doing when he chose a gun-free zone. But heck, what do I know … I've just lived it. Perhaps he would have messed his pants if he'd known I was carrying a concealed gun right there beside him in that news studio. There were no signs telling me I couldn't carry there, and I found myself walking alone that night after the interview back to my car in the side parking lot.

There are millions of gun owners in the US that have never harmed anyone with their guns. These gun grabbers need to wake up and realize that assault is a behavior, not an object.

CHAPTER 7

My Thoughts on Carrying Guns and Gun Laws

MY FIRST EXPERIENCE BEING around guns was when I was a young girl. My father was a history buff and one of his hobbies was "living history" or "re-enactments" of the French and Indian War. Our family spent many a weekend at Fort Loudon dressed in our eighteenth-century garb to entertain and educate tourists that came to visit the fort. My father and brother were British soldiers while my mother, sister and I wore our long shirts, long skirts and corsets. I didn't care for it all that much until I got to be a teenager and some cute Indian boys started coming out to the fort to re-enact in their loin cloths. Then I thought it was suddenly cool. My dad had several black powder rifles and I used to sit in his workshop in the garage and watch him clean and work on them.

Here I am with my dad, brother and sister at Fort
Loudon in 1993.

Some people cringe at the thought of a child being around firearms. Accidents with guns are a common concern with many in the public. Accidental gun-related deaths do occur in the United States. In 2007, the latest year for which numbers are available from the Centers for Disease Control, 613 Americans of all ages died from accidental gun shots, though it was a tiny fraction of the 123,706 Americans who died from any type of accidental death that year.

What might scare families the most though are accidents involving young children. In 2007 only 39 children of the 41 million under age ten died of accidental gun shots. Every one of these accidents are tragic, but with 124 million adults and around half of the children living in households with guns, a little perspective is helpful. With 41 million children under age ten in the US, it is hard to think of any other item that is as commonly owned in American homes, that is as potentially as lethal, that has as low of an accidental death rate. About 30 children a year drown in water buckets. The Centers for Disease Control reported in 2007 that 65 children died from poisonings, 637 from drownings, 1,150 from suffocations, and 1,190 from accidental motor vehicle deaths.

There are a lot of misconceptions about accidental gun deaths involving children. These deaths rarely involve "naturally curious" children shooting other children. From 1995 to 2001 only about nine of these accidental gun deaths each year involve a child under 10 shooting another child or themselves. Overwhelmingly, these shooters are adult males who have long histories of alcoholism, arrests for violent crimes, automobile crashes, and suspended or revoked driver's licenses.

Even if gun locks can stop the few children who abuse a gun from doing so, gun locks cannot stop adults from firing their own gun. The real risk is from people having a violent criminal record or a history of substance abuse, not from them having a gun.

Research in academic journals such as the *Journal of Law and Economics* shows that convincing parents not to own guns or to at least lock them up will cost more lives than it will save. It also gives a misleading impression of what poses the greatest dangers to children. As locked guns are less accessible, it also causes more crime as criminals have less to worry about if they attack defenseless victims. Criminals are also much more successful in the crimes that they do commit.

ۼ ۼ ۼ

CARRYING A GUN DOES NOT MAKE YOU INVINCIBLE. I LEARNED of Massad Ayoob (internationally known firearms and self-defense instructor) when I started doing interviews with Mark Walters on *Armed American Radio*. I listened to a few of his interviews and decided I needed to purchase his book *In the Gravest Extreme*. As I read his book I could see that this was someone who had advice that every gun owner should hear. Massad talks about how many people (especially those who have high amounts of testosterone running through their veins) who start carrying a gun suddenly feel somewhat invincible and how dangerous that can be.

Ayoob states, "Civilians who buy guns for street defense tend to think that their very possession will alleviate the dangers that made them afraid to walk through a certain area may, after he buys a gun and acquires a carry permit, go back to walking through that area. After all, he reasons, isn't it safe for him to go where he pleases now that he packs a gun?" Massad goes on to say that you should never do this, because a prosecutor in a self-defense shooting case may ask why you would choose to do that and whether you were just looking for a justifiable reason to shoot someone. This will NOT look good in a courtroom and you never want to take the chance of the jury coming back with a verdict that lands you in prison for many years.

I agree with Massad and I don't ever want to go looking for trouble or put myself in a potentially dangerous situation. It is just not worth it. I have family and friends that I love seeing and I never want to have to see them through bars or perhaps not see them at all because I am six feet under. We have to be responsible for ourselves and make good, sound decisions while we are "packing." Now, having said that, if I have taken precautionary measures to not put myself in danger and danger finds me anyway, well, that is a different story.

I of course do not EVER want to have to shoot someone. I don't carry my gun to kill anyone, I carry it so that I can survive. We now have sensible legislation here in Tennessee called "Stand Your Ground." This was made law in 2007 and says the following .

> Notwithstanding the provisions of § 39-17-1322, a person who is not engaged in unlawful activity and is in a place where such person has a right to be has no duty to retreat before threatening or using force against another person when and to the degree the person reasonably believes the force is immediately necessary to protect against the other's use or attempted use of unlawful force.

As my friend, Skip Coryell, states about the "Stand Your Ground" concept in his book (*Blood in the Streets*) "In simple terms, this means that we don't have to run from the bad guys anymore. We can stand our ground and fight to protect our families and ourselves. What kind of twisted, warped society mandates that its citizens must run from rapists, murderers, and thieves or face possible criminal and civil prosecution? Now I'm just a greasy, old, redneck, bow hunting, Marine, but that just don't make no sense to me."

غ غ غ

It was not until I was about 24 years old and met a United States Marine sniper that I really thought about my own personal safety and became interested in learning to shoot. He trained me on handgun safety and took me to the range. You can't get much better training than from a Jarhead Sniper! I started out with a .22 competition semi-auto and a revolver. Once I had a handle on that, I moved to a .38 revolver and a .9mm semi-auto. I learned a great deal from him, and I will always appreciate that he opened my eyes to the importance of self-defense. I continued my training on my own for several years and decided to try my hand at a shooting competition in 2007.

Ladies Day Shoot with the
Second Amendment Sisters in 2007

It was at this competition that I met a man who would be one of my firearms instructors. He was the owner of a security academy and had been a police officer for over 30 years. He was known around town for disarming a bomb back in his younger days when he was on the bomb squad and nuts enough to do something like that! I told Ben that I was going to go through the steps to get a handgun carry permit and he was so excited for me that he bought me a Smith and Wesson .38 Airweight revolver for my birthday.

I went to the academy to get my permit training. I was taught handgun functionality, gun safety, maintenance, justifiable use of force, defensive mindset and self defense shooting skills. I enjoyed this class so much that I volunteered to help at the range after I got my carry permit. I received my permit on April 2, 2008 (exactly one year to the day before Ben was killed).

When it was needed, I volunteered to help on the range. My husband was very supportive of me volunteering and taking the steps to protect myself. Ben actually told me about a lady he used to work with whose daughter was found strangled to death in the back of a parked car. Ben told me, "Babe I am so glad you carry that gun!" I thought about what my husband had told me, and I paid close attention to every lecture that was given on self-defense. At the range, I enjoyed working with others who were getting their own carry permits and I especially liked working with other women.

There was one day at the range that I met a woman I will never forget. This woman was probably in her midfifties, attractive, had perfect hair, pressed clothes, perfectly painted nails and was paying very close attention, but she was very scared and was on the verge of tears while in firearms training. The firearms instructors worked with her patiently and by the end of the day she was shooting with confidence and was "on target." I later learned that this woman had been brutally beaten and raped just months prior.

I left the range that day feeling horrible for her, but at the same time feeling great that she would now be able to defend herself. She now had "The Great Equalizer" in her hands and the training to stop a rapist in his tracks. She is now a rapist's worst nightmare, instead of an easy target. We women are at a disadvantage physically when it comes to defending ourselves even against an unarmed male the same size as us. We are simply not as strong as most men physically. Having a gun that you are trained to use for self-defense puts a woman on "equal footing" if she is faced with an attacker. I applaud her for taking the necessary steps to protect herself in the future and refusing to be a victim again.

Gun Turn-in Programs

I READ AN ARTICLE ABOUT HOW THE FORMER "GOVERNATOR" of California "Arnold Schwarzenegger" joined Stockton city officials in kicking off a program that offered gift certificates for guns. The article said gangs and gun violence had plagued the city and 30 of its 42 homicides to date involved guns. They were encouraging mothers, fathers and other relatives to turn in guns their kids may have hidden under mattresses or in closets. Well, as my friend Ramona so eloquently said regarding this article, "Call me crazy, but if your gang-banger kid is hiding guns under their mattress then maybe they need to be turning in their kid and not just the gun!"

If the governor wanted to "Terminate Violence," why didn't he make "ethics and character education" a mandatory course in public schools? How about we allow kids to actually pray in school? How about we actually start disciplining kids again instead of suing teachers that discipline? While these gun-turn-in programs make some people feel warm and fuzzy, law enforcement knows that this is just a tactic to make the public feel safer. These gangbangers are not going to turn in their guns. The majority of these guns that are turned in come from the kind of people that you don't need to worry about in the first place and the guns are most likely old and not functional anyway. I'm certainly not going to turn over my $500 gun for a $25 or $50 gift certificate. Come on! Get real!

Banning Guns

THEN THERE ARE PEOPLE WHO WANT TO BAN GUNS AND WILL use stories of how young children have been killed in gun accidents by finding their parent's gun and playing with it. It's a terrible thing for a child to die no matter how it happens. Like I said before, more children die from car accidents and swimming pool accidents than from gun accidents. Yet I don't see the Million Mom March or the Brady Campaign wanting to ban vehicles and swimming pools.

These people want to blame the gun (an object) instead of blaming behavior. The parents should have never left a gun out for a child to get a hold of. I have heard suicide used as an argument against guns. Well, a person can kill themself with over-the-counter drugs too, but I don't see those on the ban list. You can kill yourself pretty easily with a rope, but I don't see a push to ban rope from being sold at the local Home Depot. You can run your car off a bridge, and somehow I don't see cars or bridges being blamed.

There are people out there that honestly believe that guns are the problem and that guns cause crime. As Ted Nugent has said "If guns cause crime, then my guns are defective."

There are millions of gun owners in the US that have never harmed anyone with their guns. Gun grabbers need to wake up and realize that assault is a behavior, not an object.

Sportscaster Bob Costas took it upon himself during Sunday Night Football to let millions of viewers know they should blame the gun when Kansas City Chiefs football player Jovan Belcher decided to shoot and kill his girlfriend "Kasandra Perkins" and then kill himself using a handgun in 2012. The call for more gun control immediately started again because of one man's evil choice with a particular tool. A tool that could have very easily been a knife or his bare hands instead. Believe me, if Jovan Belcher had never owned a gun in his life, he and his girlfriend would be just as dead. The shear magnitude of his stature and strength far outweighed his girlfriend. I just wonder, if Kasandra had her own handgun for self defense, would she still be alive today to raise her child. It wasn't long after the Belcher murder/suicide that Dallas Cowboys player "Josh Brent" was arrested for intoxication manslaughter after deciding to drink and drive, wrecked and rolled the vehicle, killing his teammate "Jerry Brown" in the passenger seat. Yet Bob Costas was not seen calling for bans on vehicles or alcohol. Based on Costas's line of thinking, everyone should be blaming the vehicle and alcohol while ignoring the person who made the poor decision. Blame the object not the person, right Bob?

The mainstream media has a habit of always reporting on horrible events carried out by a madman with a gun. Do guns make it easier for bad people to do bad things? Yes. I surely know that for a fact. Do guns make it easier for good people to defend themselves against those bad people? Absolutely. Ben's murderer did not have a criminal record, he didn't even have a parking ticket in his history. He had never been diagnosed with a mental illness and was able to purchase a gun legally. The only way you can stop someone like this from harming others, is to have a good guy with a gun present and trained to stop him.

What the liberal media fails to report on is how many innocent lives are saved because a good person had a gun. Justified self defense with a gun happens everyday, and is far more prevalent than the criminal use of guns that are pumped through the boobtube, internet or papers for us to absorb. In order to get an idea of just how many of these stories actually exist, you would have to go to websites that share stories of lawful self defense like *The NRA's Armed Citizen*, *Guns Save Lives* and *Gun Owners of America*. The media would have you believe that these situations are rare when in fact they are not. Studies have been done on self defense cases across the nation, and the ratio for self defense use of a firearm compared to criminal use is 5 to 1. You will never hear that from CNN, MSNBC, ABC, CBS, etc.

Their agenda is to have you fear guns and believe that guns cause crime. The best way you can defend yourself and your loved ones is to have the best defensive tool possible – a firearm. However, if you are going to have a firearm, you should take it upon yourself as a responsible citizen to get trained on justifiable use of force, safety and self defense shooting skills. There is no such thing as too much training. There are certified firearms trainers in every city of every state in this nation. Go get yourself trained if you choose to have a gun.

What about the Police?

MANY PEOPLE BELIEVE THAT IT IS THE POLICE THAT WILL PROtect them should they ever need help. I have a great appreciation for law enforcement and the risks they take every day to try and protect citizens. However, they have no constitutional duty to do so as proven in many a Supreme Court case.

Never has an individual citizen ever won one of these cases.

One case in particular was of a woman in Castle Rock, Colorado who had an order of protection taken out on her estranged husband who was known to be violent. The lawsuit was for the failure of the police to respond to the woman's pleas for help after her estranged husband violated a protective order by kidnapping their three young daughters, whom he eventually killed. The Supreme Court conclusion about the responsibility of police for the security of your family and loved ones is as follows:

"You, and only you, are responsible for your security and the security of your family and loved ones."

ۓ ۓ ۓ

CHRISTMAS 2009 WAS VERY DIFFICULT. IT WAS MY FIRST Christmas without my husband. I had this great new job that I was really excited about at the Capitol, but it was the holidays and I was missing my husband something awful. Governor Phil Bredesen and the First Lady were holding their annual "A Tennessee Season to Remember" event at the Capitol for families of homicide victims.

The First Lady, Andrea Conte, had been a victim of crime back in 1988. She was beaten and dragged into a car in the parking lot of her business. The perpetrator drove off with her in what could have been truly disastrous. She was surprisingly able to fight him off and jump from the car. The kidnapper got away and the following year this same man killed a woman in a Nashville park.

At this event, we would bring pictures of our deceased family members and put them in an ornament to be displayed on the Christmas wreaths at the Capitol throughout the holiday season. When I went into the house chamber I was immediately met by one of the first lady's private security state troopers who sat with me through the entire event. I noticed that no other grieving family members were personally escorted by armed security other than myself. This trooper even walked with me while I walked past the governor and first lady to place Ben's picture on the wreath.

I had been very verbal about my support for right to carry laws and disappointed in his veto of the restaurant carry bill but never had I ever threatened someone and especially not the governor. If someone does that, they get arrested rather quickly. I was a known permit holder and a staffer who spoke her mind on her own time about issues of public interest regarding self defense and the Second Amendment. The Trooper was very nice but it was humiliating to me in a time when I just wanted to honor my loved one like everyone else. Anytime you take a firm stance on gun rights, you will be met with those who think you may be violent or a just a plain ole' nut. It is really unfair but it is just another thing I have learned to deal with. I have no idea who had the trooper stay alongside me like that or if it was just a rare coincidence.

"Predator vs. Prey. I know who you are, run. Where will you work where I can't find you? At home, at dinner, in your sleep, every f***ing waking moment. This is going to be very painful. You've pissed me off now. You are about to see my bad side. What kind of life do you have now?! You are forever un-forgiven."

CHAPTER 8

Stalking His Prey

LAW-ABIDING CITIZENS ARE THE ones who have to foot the bill (pay taxes) to keep offenders in prison. Violent offenders should stay in there for many years so they can soak up all that iron and concrete and maybe think twice about harming someone again. We need to start using "truth in sentencing laws" all across the nation for violent offenders. These prisoners should all have to work to give back to society as well. I am a huge fan of hard labor for these prisoners. It needs to be unpleasant enough so they will never want to commit another crime and be sent back to a prison.

Now let's get to the hard-core violent offenders (murderers). As far as I am concerned, if you intentionally murder someone then you should face the death penalty, PERIOD. I know there are some cases where innocent people have been put to death in the past and therefore some people are against the death penalty. This occurred before DNA testing and other forensic analysis was so advanced.

There are also those who believe the death penalty is cruel and inhumane and we as a society should be above that. Well, if those people have such a problem with it then maybe they will open up their own home for these murderers to come live at their house with their own family.

Those murderers sure were not ABOVE that when they decided to kill some innocent person, now were they? I don't want to pay for them to be fed and housed for the rest of their lives and I shouldn't have to! In cases where the evidence is solid, death should be without question. When I say solid I mean: DNA match, finger- print match, murder weapon, murder on film, witnesses, victim's body, confession, etc. When the evidence is absolute (as it was for my husband's killer) then as soon as that murderer is found guilty after their fair trial, he/she should be able to have one year for comprehensive appeal.

After that they should be taken out behind the courthouse and have a bullet put in their head. DONE. A bullet is astronomically cheaper, simpler and more reliable than the expensive components and procedure of lethal injection. Instead, the perpetrators have more rights than the victims. Often times the victim dies a painful, cruel death and the killer get's to be put down in a peaceful, humane way. I believe if we went back to the days of public executions, crime would plummet. There must be justice that is severe, swift, and certain.

The Evidence

BEN'S MURDERER WROTE A BLOG ON MYSPACE.COM THE DAY before he carried out his plan. I did not learn of this blog until the local news found it and reported on it the day after Ben was killed. The blog said the following:

"Predator vs. Prey. I know who you are, run. Where will you work where I can't find you? At home, at dinner, in your sleep, every f***ing waking moment. This is going to be very painful. You've pissed me off now. You are about to see my bad side. What kind of life do you have now?! You are forever un-forgiven."

There is also a security video of Ben's murder. I had no idea that the restaurant we were running karaoke out of even had a surveillance video system, until the detectives told me. I was also told how lucky I was to have this evidence, because the restaurant was having problems with the surveillance system just a week before (it was not working). They had someone come out and fix it just days prior to Ben's murder.

So not only is there a blog that establishes pre-meditation, but there is also a video of this man executing Ben. There are also the items found in the killer's truck that night. Again, this establishes pre-meditation.

I also did my own investigative work. I paid $50 to run a background check on Ben's killer. I found every city in every state where he had lived. I decided to send the news report with his mug shot to all of the newspapers in these towns. I knew by what I had studied in my psychology courses in college, that stalking behavior does not just pop up for someone in their midforties.

This man had to have stalked other women in his past and I aimed to find them. *The Rocket Miner Newspaper* in Rock Springs, Wyoming decided to run the story with his mug shot on the front page. This man was raised in that town and went to that high school. I knew if there was someone else this man had stalked and if she saw the newspaper, surely she would try to get in contact with me.

It wasn't but three weeks after the story ran that I got the phone call. To preserve her privacy, I will call her Mary. She and her husband moved into the same neighborhood as Ben's killer and his then-wife in the mid 1990s in Rock Springs, Wyoming. They were actually next-door neighbors. Mary told of how they got to know this couple and became friends with them. They would hang out together while going fishing, hunting and grilling out.

Mary was the kind of neighbor that would cook for the whole community. She liked to make cinnamon rolls and she would take them to all her neighbors. Mary believes this is when the stalking started. This man apparently took her kindness as "flirting." He believed the cinnamon rolls were really for him only and Mary giving them to the others neighbors was just something she did as cover.

He started to take an eerie interest in Mary. He would make it a point to be in his driveway first thing in the morning when Mary would leave for work. When she got home in the evening, he would be there to stare at her again. He would pretend he was working on his car or on the house, but she would always catch him gawking at her. Mary told her husband about this and he just laughed it off as an innocent crush. When Mary would get up in the morning and get ready to leave, her husband would say, "Awww … look honey, your boyfriend is out there waiting on ya!" It was a joke to him. This man had called Mary's office several times and left his name with the secretary, but Mary never called him back. He then left her a CD on her doorstep of the Michael Peterson song *From here to eternity*.

It had gone from what Mary's husband thought was an innocent crush to really creeping Mary out and she couldn't take it anymore. Mary's husband was of little help because he did not take it seriously. Mary asked several of her friends what they would do in her shoes, and they all said she should gently inform his wife of everything he is doing behind her back. At this point Mary was pregnant with her second child and this man was still acting creepy toward her. Mary finally told the wife everything her husband had been doing. The wife went back and confronted her husband, and he turned it all around to make it sound like Mary was actually the one pursuing him. The wife believed her husband and it destroyed the women's friendship.

After Mary had the baby she started working out to lose the baby weight she had gained. Her stalker neighbor noticed her faithfully going to the gym and decided to buy a treadmill. He put it in the front room window with the blinds open.

The wife still remained in denial that her own husband was pursuing another woman right under her own nose. I learned that the wife divorced Ben's killer some years later. Perhaps she had finally figured him out. Mary ended up moving to another state and within a year or so of her moving, guess who showed up at her front doorstep knocking at her door? He had apparently traveled a very long distance and found her.

She got her kids in the back bedroom and they stayed there until he went away. When she checked the front door, she found a note. Mary can't remember now what it said but she does know she threw it away that night. She never saw him again, until she saw his mug shot in the paper that her friend sent her from Wyoming. Mary ended up going on the local Fox channel here in Nashville via live-feed audio/video from Arizona. Both of our interviews were used in a news segment talking about the dangers of stalkers. I sent the news report to the detectives working our case. I don't know if it did any good other than to show that this guy apparently had a thing for married women and was a weirdo for many years.

The one thing that kept me going and gave me purpose was my Second Amendment advocacy work. It gave me a healthy outlet to try and educate others about protecting themselves and their families. My story had been in the local papers, local news and was now going national.

CHAPTER 9

The Frustrating Prelude to the Trial

BEN SUPPORTED THE DEATH PEN-
alty and so do I. Unfortunately, there are people
in this country who aim to see it abolished in
order to save money or for moral reasons. In California, a
huge debate has been going on about ending the death penalty because of multi-billion dollar budget deficits. There are
over seven hundred inmates in that state sitting on death row
and the argument is that it costs the taxpayers an exorbitant
amount of money. I personally believe our capital punishment system should be overhauled, so that these condemned
prisoners do not spend 20-plus years sitting around awaiting
death. The execution chemicals used in lethal injection are
extremely costly. We could alleviate these costs by going
back to using other less costly methods of terminating these
monsters. A single bullet costs about one dollar. It is also
time to end this long, drawn-out system of appeals these
killers are allowed. California gave a one-million-dollar, tax-
payer-funded heart transplant to an inmate serving 14 years

for robbery while five hundred law-abiding Californians waited for hearts. Genius I tell you! Genius! Legislators around the nation need to make reforming capital punishment a priority, and we need to stop allowing incredibly stupid things to be done with our money!

> *"If we execute murderers and there is in fact no deterrent effect, we have killed a bunch of murderers. If we fail to execute murderers, and doing so would in fact have deterred other murders, we have allowed the killing of a bunch of innocent victims. I would much rather risk the former. This, to me, is not a tough call."*
>
> *– John McAdams*

I was told early on by the prosecutor that he will not seek the death penalty for our case, because it simply did not fit the criteria. He also said that it could take up to 15 years before all the appeals were over with if he did get death and that is hard on families. There are 15 points of criteria that would make someone eligible for the death penalty, and only one has to be met here in Tennessee to pursue it. I believe there were two criteria met in this case. Number one is, was the death cruel? Well, I'd say someone being shot six times with a .45 caliber in front of their spouse is pretty damn cruel don't you!? The second is, were other people's lives put in danger at the time of the murder? Well that's a no brainer! There were 50 people in the restaurant with multiple shots fired!

Fighting for the death penalty is up to the prosecutor and how they choose to interpret the law and if they are willing to based on the facts. In my unprofessional opinion, the death penalty could have been put on the table in this case had the prosecutor wanted to. This could have been used as a bargaining chip for an admission of guilt and an agreement to take a life sentence. This would have kept me from going through a very painful murder trial and would have kept this dangerous man off our streets forever. That option was apparently never seriously considered.

There were three mental evaluations done on Ben's murderer and it took over three years to go to trial. How cruel is it to the victim's family to have to sit and wait that long for justice? How can they expect a witness's memory to be any good after that length of time? So much for the "swift and speedy" trial that is referred to in our US Constitution. His state-appointed defense attorney tried to get him off with an "insanity defense." The tactics used in the courtroom were beyond mind-numbing for me, Ben's children, our friends and family.

Using Psychology to Deflect Guilt

OUR CRIMINAL JUSTICE SYSTEM WANTS TO KNOW WHY someone kills. They want to get in the killer's mind and try to figure them out. In our case, the fact that he did it was clear, but that wasn't enough; they wanted to delve into his mental state. Is he a psychopath, paranoid–delusional, insane, multiple personality disorder, erotomaniac, etc.?

Let's face it, these monsters can be pretty smart. They will sit there and make up all kinds of crazy stories if they think it will keep them from facing justice, i.e., death or a very long prison sentence. They have all the time in the world to sit in their little cell and dream up anything and everything. I studied psychology and I don't give a flying flip what his mental state was or is. One of the most notorious serial killers in Tennessee is sitting on death row and has consistently stated that his killing was due to "scientific technology." He claims the government was controlling his mind and actions, causing him to commit this crime. These killers try everything they can to play the system to either appear incompetent or insane.

It was about two years after Ben's murder that I got a letter from Ben's murderer. Yes, the monster actually wrote me a letter from jail. As if this monster hadn't put me through enough already, he suddenly thought it would be bright to write me! I was in shock when my attorney told me that the killer had sent a letter to his office, addressed to me. I said, "How in the hell can a murderer be allowed to write their victim a freakin' letter!"

My attorney had no other explanation other than it was marked as confidential and addressed on the envelope to his law office. He held onto the letter for about a month and struggled with telling me about it but said legally he had to. I just sat there thinking, *That son of a bitch is working hard to do what he can to appear insane and I bet his defense attorney put him up to doing it.*

I asked my attorney if the letter appeared to be "insane." He said, "Yes, Nikki it does and I am sorry I have to tell you that it is here. If you don't want to see it, I can throw it away." Now most people would probably say, "Nikki, just throw the damn thing away." But stop and think if it was your loved one that was murdered, would you want to see what was in the letter? I had questions that needed answering, and I thought perhaps the letter would offer something, anything.

Well, it didn't. To me, the letter seemed to be written by someone stuck in a concrete room, working overtime trying to sound like he was as nutty as all get out. Nothing in the letter made any sense. It just sounded like a very detailed, fabricated story line for a really twisted movie on Lifetime. Several months later I would get yet another letter which again offered nothing but did however keep me from sleeping and started the flashback nightmares again. I finally told my attorney to destroy any other letters he sent as I did not want to see them.

Justice

FOR THE FIRST YEAR AFTER BEN'S DEATH WHEN I TRIED TALK-ing to the prosecutor, I perceived him as condescending and he seemed annoyed that he had to deal with me. Granted, I was asking many questions and had concerns as I had never been through anything like this and did not fully understand criminal law and how it all worked. Victims and their families naturally want to know what is going on as their lives have been forever altered and, in some cases, completely shattered. The one thing that kept me going and gave me purpose was my Second Amendment advocacy work. It gave me a healthy outlet to try and educate others about protecting themselves and their family. My story had been in the local papers, local news and was now going national.

I'll never forget one day in court when there was a discussion period that I attended. The prosecutor talked to me in one of the side rooms about what was going on in the case. He told me that the defense was doing a mental evaluation on the guy. I already knew of the evidence in the man's truck, because the prosecutor let me look in his binder full of papers regarding the case. I had run across the search warrant and was shocked when I saw that Ben's killer had two more guns (shotgun and rifle), ammo, a baseball bat, binoculars, gloves, rope and a knife. I asked the prosecutor about the evidence found in the murderer's truck and why he thought those items were there. He seemed annoyed that I'd brought it up and said, "Well, let's just hope nobody finds out about that."

I sat there very confused as to why he would not want

anyone to know about the evidence. I asked him why he thought this man would have two more guns in his truck that night. His face turned bright red and he said angrily, "Nikki, I don't know why he had those guns in his truck! Maybe he's just a gun nut! I hate guns! I don't understand why anyone would want to own a gun!" That is when I realized that this man had been condescending with me all these months for a reason.

I was extremely concerned at this point that the man the courts had appointed to seek justice for Ben and I was someone who might despise all the advocacy work I had been doing for Second Amendment rights. This scared me. I started talking to my friends and family about the political and personal bias comments he had made to me and they felt concerned as well. I had heard stories of professors at universities picking on conservative students, but I had never heard about an attorney provided by the state doing something like that.

I tried talking to some ladies who used to work for the Davidson County Court to see if they could get me a meeting with the District Attorney General but every attempt I made failed. I tried calling his office several times to see if I could speak to him with no luck but let his secretary know my concerns and my contact info. After waiting for months and hearing nothing, I determined he did not want to speak with me.

ۉ ۉ ۉ

ONE DAY I CALLED THE PROSECUTOR TO CHECK ON HOW THINGS were coming along. It had been many months since I'd last spoken with him and I needed an update. I left a voicemail and he called me back. The prosecutor said that the defense had the murderer evaluated and the psychologist was saying that, at the time of the offense, they believe he could have been suffering from a mental illness, and they are diagnosing him as paranoid–delusional.

The prosecutor said to me, "Nikki, he was never stalking you. He is just a nut case. The guy is out of his mind." As I listened on the other end of the phone, I began to realize that this man who was suppose to be on "our side" was actually siding with the defense and was openly admitting it! I thought, *How is this person going to insure we get a fair and transparent shot at justice when he has already formed his own opinion and sided with the defense?*

He proceeded to tell me how Ben's murderer told the psychologist that he and his girlfriend in Florida had broken up. Ben's murderer said that the ex-girlfriend had a family member who was a police officer and that the officers in that department would constantly pull him over for no reason. He told the psychologist that he felt there was a huge conspiracy by the Florida police department to "get him."

The murderer then moved to Nashville but then said that the Nashville Police Department was in on the conspiracy plan also, and somehow my husband was in on the plan. He told the psychologist something about pictures being taken of him by patrons in the karaoke restaurants and that my husband, who must have been in on the conspiracy with the cops, was posting them on websites. He told the psychologist that a woman in the restaurant had once made a throat-slash gesture to him and that he thought people wanted to kill him. Ben's murderer said that Ben had written a blog about him to rally people up against him. When the detectives asked him if he had actually seen the blog he said, "No. But I know it's there."

I interrupted the prosecutor and told him, "This is all

bullshit! That man is just making up crazy scenarios to appear insane!" I tried explaining to the prosecutor again how this man was stalking me and how all this other nonsense was made up garbage, and there was no proof of any of this nonsense the murderer was spewing. I had never seen anyone be mean to that guy in the restaurant let alone make some kind of threat.

I reminded him that what could be proven were: the Myspace messages he sent me; the bartenders that said he showed up at the karaoke restaurants I worked at downtown; that he ordered a beer in each place but never drank it and just sat there waiting and waiting; the killer asking one of the bartenders downtown how to get to Jonny's; the blog he wrote the day before; the items in his truck and the fact that he shot and killed Ben!

Then he said, "Nikki, here is how insane he really is. He does not even want to use the insanity defense, and his family does not want him to either because they are concerned it will make the family look bad."

I didn't even know what to say but I blurted out, "Look bad?! They don't want their family to look bad?! Are you freakin' kidding me?! He murdered my husband in cold blood! What the hell is wrong with his family!?" I thought *Boy, the apple doesn't fall far from the tree does it.* I was growing more concerned with every mention of the word "insane" from this prosecutor.

I'd left several messages for the District Attorney General, but several more months went by and still I heard nothing from him. I figured my concerns with the prosecutor would fall on deaf ears anyway. I assumed they were all buddies and they were going to watch each other's back no matter what. I decided to call the prosecutor at this point and let him know that I was not happy with him. Before I could say anything he briskly said, "I don't appreciate you having your buddies call up here saying things about me!"

It was at that point that I lost it and let him have an ear full. I was at my boiling point and beyond angry. I am a nice lady but I do have a point when my inner bitch can take over. Don't be fooled guys, all women have an inner bitch, even the really sweet ones, and especially the southern ones! I dug into him some more and hung up. He ended up being much nicer to me and apologized the next time I saw him for the next discussion period. I'm pretty sure he thought he was dealing with Satan after the way I spoke to him. I apologized also even though I really felt I was justified in being upset but realized I could have toned down my rather eloquent "language of the sea."

I think sometimes prosecutors and the entire court system are guilty of forgetting about victims and their families, because they deal with this madness all the time and become immune to it. They forget the devastation that criminals bring on good folks and how hard it can be to deal with from day to day. To flip the coin, I'm sure it's not easy for them to deal with furious, distraught victims either. It makes me that much more unforgiving of the criminals that put us in this position. The court system tries to cater to victims by having a Victim Witness Coordinator, but God bless the good woman who was assigned to me as coordinator because I was just not having it. It seemed all the questions I had could only be answered by the prosecutor and I'd have to wait for her to contact him to ask and then get back to me. I finally just thought "forget this, I just need to talk to the prosecutor!" It was wasting my time and hers, but she and I actually got along.

However, I did fear the prosecutor's own personal feelings of disgust with me and my beliefs on gun rights. I was concerned it could hinder the case, and that the Criminal Justice System might fail Ben and I because he may not do all he should on the case. I did not want to see that monster who murdered my husband get out of prison in my lifetime. I knew if he ever did get out, then I would have to look over my shoulder constantly wondering if he was following me again, aiming to hurt me or someone else.

Not long before the trial date that I had been waiting years for, I finally heard from the District Attorney General's Office saying he would meet with me. I thought, *Great! After all this time and now here we are almost going to trial and now you want to meet with me when it's too late to try and get another prosecutor?* By this point, I was worn down and worn out from all the waiting. I believed it would no longer be worth my time trying to raise my concerns about the prosecutor as I did not want anything postponing the trial that had already taken so long to finally get to.

My father went with me to the meeting, and, as soon as I walked in, I noticed the prosecutor had come to the meeting also. My father and I spoke with them about what to expect in the trial and what the strategy was. I never raised my concerns as it was apparent to me that these two men were playing on the same team and I didn't stand a chance. It was pretty obvious to me that it was not a coincidence that this meeting was held just before the trial instead of when I initially called. I was powerless to try and have anything changed now and they knew it.

I could not believe that this judge was actually going to let this person walk free amongst us in society one day. I thought our criminal justice system was supposed to protect society as a whole?

CHAPTER 10

The Trial

AFTER THE TRIAL HAD BEEN pushed back seven times, and after waiting for over three years, the day I would face Ben's murderer finally came.

I was not able to sleep but a few hours the night before the trial. I had prepared my victim impact statement and read it to myself eight times before I could pull it off without crying. I did not want to show any hint of weakness to Ben's murderer in that courtroom. I refused to allow myself to cry in front of him.

There were about 20 friends and family in the courtroom with me that day, including Ben's two oldest daughters from his previous marriage. Ben's girls were always more like friends to me instead of step daughters. The three of us sat next to one another for what ended up being a three-day long battle over mental illness and guilt.

The local news had come and set up in the corner of the

courtroom and was there throughout the entire trial. My father was livid it had taken so long for this case to come to trial after the court had so much solid evidence for so many years. He had seen firsthand how difficult all the waiting had been on me. I had finally just come to accept the delays after realizing that victims come last and all this waiting was based on mental evaluations and attorneys dragging their feet. It's just another day at the office for them.

I hate to be that blunt about it, but if anything ever happens to either yourself or your loved ones, you'd better grow some thick skin quick. I'm not going to paint a pretty picture for you because it is hell. It is a long and drawn out, painful process and many times you feel totally lost. The court system sees so many victims and so many violent incidents that often they simply forget the real hurt and anguish that those victims face. It is routine for them.

It literally feels like picking a number and sitting down to wait your turn similar to going to the Department of Motor Vehicles to get your driver's license. You are just another number. That's what it felt like for me. The perpetrator's rights and consideration for him/her will always come first. They even get to choose whether they want a jury or not.

Ben's killer chose to have no jury. He wanted a bench trial (judge only). I remember the prosecutor telling me this and I thought we should push back and insist on the opposite (a jury). After all, why would I want to go along with what that piece of human excrement wanted?! But the prosecutor felt the bench trial would work better. As I knew nothing about the justice system, I had to trust him. They at least throw you a crumb and make you as the victim feel like you have some kind of say, but you ultimately don't. It's really up to the attorneys. It's not a justice system; it's just a system. You'll see why as I get further into the trial.

Day One

DAY ONE CONSISTED OF HEARING FROM THE WITNESSES, IN-cluding myself. Normally, witnesses are not allowed to stay in the courtroom while other witnesses testify. I was allowed to stay for all testimony because I was a victim also. A handful of witnesses took the stand and identified Ben's murderer. I took the stand and was handed copies of the Myspace messages Ben's killer had sent me years ago before I'd deleted and blocked him. To my amazement, the messages were not in chronological order and the messages were cut off at the end where someone had copied them pretty poorly. The prosecutor asked me to read the messages. I tried reading them but nothing was in order and I could not make sense of it because parts were cut off and it had been years since I saw this stuff. I sat there thinking, _"You mean to tell me I have waited for three years and you brilliant attorneys couldn't get your act together well enough to even get this info straight!?"_ It made we wonder if the prosecutor had literally just opened the binder on this case the day before to prepare for the trial.

The prosecutor then asked me to read one specific message where Ben's murderer asked me if Ben had moved out because he saw a message from me on my friend Kimberly's wall that said "get out." I then explained to the court that my friend Kimberly had been going through something in her personal life at that time and I was telling her to get out of a relationship. The prosecutor asked why he would think that Ben was gone. I explained that he apparently was looking on my friends pages for comments by me and associating something totally unrelated with my husband. I thought this was a really stupid move on the prosecutor's part. Why would he specifically pick out a section for me to read that would leave the impression that this guy was associating unrelated things and appearing delusional? I'm no attorney but I believe I would have been happy to ignore that part. Unless of course, I wanted to sabotage the thing so the defense could have an edge.

I told the court that I was happily married and that it was my belief that this man was stalking me. The prosecutor just said, "Yes, I know you have said that before." Then he moved on without addressing it further. The restaurant's security video was shown to the entire court where everyone witnessed Ben being shot to death. It was shown several times and every time it was shown, I felt like it was happening all over again in living color. You could have heard a pin drop as the video played in that courtroom.

The medical examiner showed diagrams of Ben's entry and exit wounds. The detective took the stand and presented all the evidence. The items found in his truck were mentioned and the defenses explanation for why he had two more guns in his truck was because he knew the hotel he was staying at did not want guns left in the room. This would obviously show that he knew right from wrong.

They played the murderer's interrogation video. The police left the empty shoulder holster on Ben's killer throughout the taped interview. He kept putting his head down in his hands and not answering questions, being elusive and uncooperative. The police just kept asking him questions over and over and tried to make him feel like he was justified so they could drag information out of him. Amazing how this works.

After about an hour, they finally got him to admit he did kill Ben (obviously). He rambled on and on with nonsense about Ben trying to destroy his life by altering pictures of him and posting them online. My husband was a Graphics Designer and his occupation was clearly posted on his social network account for others to see. Ben's killer told detectives and psychologists that my husband was part of some large conspiracy with the killer's ex-girlfriend (living in Florida), our friends, Florida Law Enforcement and Tennessee Law Enforcement to destroy him through altered pictures, GPS tracking, internet spyware, cellphone spyware, and video and audio monitoring. Apparently people were catching on that this guy was weird and started deleting him around the time I did. He blamed his failed online friendships on Ben and Ben's friends.

Day Two

THE SECOND DAY WAS WHEN THE MURDERER'S FATHER AND SIS-ter took the stand. The purpose of them testifying was to help the defense get the murderer a verdict of "Not guilty by reason of insanity." The killer's father told of how his son was stressed as a child because of his parents' divorce when he was very young. The typical struggles that many families go through these days, yet the vast majority of us who have been through this have never murdered anyone. Father and son were not really a part of each other's lives until the killer became an adult. His father told of how his son was prone to anger and how when he get's set off, he can be a hothead.

His father told a story on the stand of how some hunting friends of his son wanted to hunt on his son's property and asked if they could. His son said no, so the hunters went to do their hunting on the property next to his. Apparently Ben's killer found shot gun shells on his side of the land and went to get his own shotgun and started shooting over the hunters heads just above the tree line in anger.

Another story was told of how his son (who was living in Florida at the time) was convinced that his girlfriend was trying to poison him with tea bags. It was told how he took these tea bags to the sheriff's office and asked to have them tested. It was said that the police did not test the bags or get back with his son. So his son's explanation for not getting any help from the police was that they must be in on it too, because his girlfriend had a family member in law enforcement.

Then his father told a story of how his son had a fish pond on his property and wanted to put a chemical in it to turn the water blue in color. His dad told him, "Son, if you put that chemical in that water, it's going to kill the algae, change the oxygen levels and ultimately kill your fish you have in there." His son proceeded to put the chemical in the pond anyway despite his father's advice and lo and behold, the fish died. He then believed that his ex-girlfriend and law enforcement had somehow poisoned his pond to kill his fish.

He told of how he had come to visit his son in jail and they would talk about what he had done to Ben. His son's explanation was that he was just trying to protect his good name. The father also talked about his son losing jobs over and over again. His son's last job was lost because he refused to take a mental evaluation at the employer's request.

Management at an Energy Company where he was employed, was made aware that their employee consistently could not get along with other employees. This is what lead to the demand for a mental evaluation or else termination. He ended up being terminated for refusing the evaluation. His property and home was soon to fall into foreclosure and it was at this point that he decided to move to Music City (Nashville, Tennessee) thinking he could possibly make it in the music industry. When he moved to Nashville, people thought him odd.

At some point about a month before Ben was murdered, Ben's killer apparently went back to his house in Florida and destroyed it. I believe they said in court that he had used a chainsaw, sledgehammer and shot the place up. After the father was told about his son murdering a man in Nashville, he visited with his son in prison. The father then made his way to his son's house in Florida that was in the process of foreclosure to get his son's things. As soon as he got to the house he saw the home was completely destroyed.

The father noticed on his son's key ring two safe-deposit box keys. One safe was in the house but the other was no-where to be found. The father looked under the house thinking that perhaps his son had put the safe under there. That is where his father said he found a complete spy center with cameras, monitors, electronics, etc., that his son had hidden. None of these points were ever substantiated with any sort of proof other than the fact that the killer's father was under oath. You would think that they could at least present pictures of the destroyed home and pictures of the supposed "spy center" under the house.

When the murderer's sister took the stand, she seemed very much in denial about what her brother had done. I can understand that. After all, who wants to believe your family member is a cold-blooded killer? The prosecutor made her read the blog her brother had written the day before he murdered Ben. She started reading it but kept stopping as if she did not want to continue. She was asked to finish reading. By the end, there was no way this woman could deny what her brother's intentions were and what he ultimately did.

Conveniently enough for her, neither she nor the rest of the murderer's family were in the courtroom to see the security video of Ben being murdered. I suppose they did not want to see it. I didn't either, but I was forced to the night of April 2, 2009 and it's now permanently etched in my mind forever. The prosecutor asked her if she talked with her brother while he was in prison about what he had done to Ben. She said that they knew they were being recorded during these visits and that her brother said that if he didn't kill Ben then Ben was going to kill him. This statement conflicted with what he told his father, that he was protecting his "good name."

What I found questionable was the fact that the defense could not find anyone else other than the killer's family (who are naturally bias) to take the stand to tell of these supposed "insane" behaviors.

No Battle of the Psychologists

USUALLY IN INSANITY TRIALS YOU WILL HAVE THE DEFENSE find a psychologist to put on the stand that will back up the insanity defense with flying colors and the prosecution's psychologist will do just the opposite. As expected, the defense psychologist diagnosed Ben's murderer as having delusional-disorder and paranoia. However, what was surprising was the prosecution's psychologist. Remember my concerns about the prosecutor?

This psychologist basically agreed with the defense that Ben's killer showed signs of having delusional-disorder and paranoia. He didn't even put up a real fight. Similar to my phone conversation with the prosecutor over a year prior, this man was agreeing with the defense.

What baffles me is the fact that these psychologists took a murderer at his word. The question should not be, What does the murderer say and how often does he say it with the ability to keep the story straight, but should rather be, Does the psychologist actually believe what the killer is saying to be true? How do you go about deciphering or measuring that? Well, according to the courts, you just believe the murderer and his family members.

There was mention of anti-psychotic drugs that were being tried on the murderer and how he was doing on those medications. It was really mind numbing sitting there and listening to all this talk about the killer. So much time and attention was spent on him compared to my husband. It was as if Ben was just an afterthought. I kept thinking to myself that this man just loves the attention he is getting right now even if it is negative.

Then to my utter amazement and disgust, the judge allowed two detailed conspiracy diagrams that Ben's murderer had drawn while undergoing mental evaluation. The diagrams had many people's names listed and all were interconnected somehow with tracking devices and law enforcement from Tennessee and Florida. Ben's name and mine were included along with many of our friends and people we did not even know. The killer's name was positioned narcissistically at the center of the diagrams with everyone else listed and connected together and arrows drawn pointing back to the killer's name.

I could understand if this diagram was found in his belongings when the police searched the hotel room he was living in just outside of Nashville the night he was arrested. But this was a diagram drawn after the fact by a man desperate to try and prove he was insane. A get-out-of-jail-free card if you must. Many of my friends and Ben's who were in the courtroom that day saw their name on those diagrams. Everyone listed had never done anything to this man but were on his made up and well thought out hit list of conspirators. It took everything I had to remain composed and not jump up to yell "This is ridiculous! Why would you allow this!"

After the diagram was shown, Ben's killer looked at me and smirked, as if to say, "Ha, I know how to play this game." This was no dummy. I learned this man had worked making very good money in management positions around high-power voltage for many years. He was a supervisor over several employees and operated heavy machinery in high-risk conditions. This was an intelligent monster who knew how to manipulate.

The true test of will power is when you are just across the room from someone who purposefully took your loved one from you. My parents raised me to love God and be kind, but never did they have a conversation with me on how to deal with something like this. I was thinking of doing things to him that I had only seen in horror movies like "Saw." My mind was racing with some of the most horrible thoughts anyone can think. I cannot even begin to describe the kind of rage I was dealing with. Then I would think, *My God Nikki, look at what this man is doing to you. This is not you. You don't think like this.*

Day Three

THE THIRD DAY CONSISTED OF CLOSING ARGUMENTS AND THE verdict. The defense insisted that Ben's murderer did not understand the wrongfulness of his actions and referred to the mental evaluations. The prosecution stated that while he may have delusional disorder, it does not excuse the fact that he killed a man in cold blood that he obviously knew this a wrongful act. This was pre-meditated murder.

He wrote the blog the day before the murder. He went downtown to several different karaoke restaurants looking for the victim and his wife. When he couldn't find them, he asked the bartender for directions to Jonny's Sports Bar. He drove a good thirty minutes to get there. He carried a gun inside the restaurant illegally and concealed. He did not come in blazing away trying to take out multiple people. He very methodically hunted down and killed one man. Concerning the items that were found in his truck: he knew certain other things were wrong, such as keeping his guns in a hotel room where they were not allowed. So the excuse of not knowing right from wrong did not fit.

The judge ended up not buying the insanity defense. Thank God. I felt an instant of relief only to be hit with a jolt of utter disappointment. What should have been first degree pre-meditated murder (which would have been a life sentence) was dropped by the judge to a lesser charge of second degree murder. In the state of Tennessee, that is only a 15 to 25 year sentence. The judge apparently put a great deal of weight on the mental evaluations and conspiracy diagrams as well as the murderer's family testimony. My fears of this monster one day again being set free on society had come true.

I could not believe that this judge was actually going to let this person walk free amongst us in society one day. I thought our criminal justice system was supposed to protect society as a whole? It crossed my mind that at least sex offenders have a registry they must be on to let the people in their community know where they live. There is no such thing as a murderer registry in my state and therefore, one day, this killer could be someone's neighbor and a huge threat to them without them ever knowing it.

You see, just like those who molest children, delusional disorder is not something that can be cured. Delusional disorder can be medicated with anti-psychotic drugs in a controlled environment, but once the offender is set loose on society, who is going to monitor them and make sure they take the medication? Ben's killer is on an anti-psychotic drug called Seroquel. This medication is prescribed for bipolar disorder, schizophrenia and other mental illnesses. The problem is that in order for the drug to be effective for delusions, the dosage must be high. With a high dosage comes problems like catatonia or feeling woozy.

A person would not be able to hold down a job while on a high dose of the medication, but if they don't take the high dose then they will be delusional again. It is like playing russian-roulette with the public. If this man is delusional, (which I doubt) then what is a free and peaceful society to do with him upon release? What happens when this man decides some other innocent person is out to get him again? Who else will this monster decide to kill?

More Delays

SENTENCING WAS DELAYED SEVERAL TIMES AFTER THE TRIAL. Ben's murderer was sent to Middle Tennessee Mental Health for an additional evaluation to make sure he was fit to stand sentencing. We had to wait for the evaluation process yet again. I had never heard of someone being evaluated for sentencing, and I wondered how much all of this was costing Tennessee tax payers.

Finally sentencing day came. All our family and friends piled into the courtroom yet again. The most I could hope for would be twenty-five years. I was called to the stand to give my victim impact statement. I did my best to convey in graphic detail the nightmare I had lived through witnessing my husband's murder. The last statement I made was to Ben's murderer. I stared at him as I said, "My husband, Ben, is more of a man in his death than you are living." His face was totally expressionless as I spoke. It was as if he did not have a soul.

I asked for the maximum sentence with no parole. I leaned into the microphone and told the court, "The fact that we are talking about anything less than a life sentence here today is just beyond me." The judge then leaned over to me and whispered, "Ms. Goeser, do I understand correctly that you work for a member of the legislature?" I replied, "Yes, Your Honor

I do." The judge then said "and you understand that I am not the one who makes the laws, I just enforce them." I replied that I understood that. In other words, he was saying, if you don't like what is going on here, talk to the people you work with and get it changed, because this is the way the law reads right now for a case like this. I could not understand why the judge lowered it from first degree to second degree. This decision had nothing to do with the legislature, it had to do with him and his decision, despite the overwhelming evidence.

A psychiatrist that worked for the mental facility Ben's killer had just been evaluated at took the stand. He told the court that they felt Seroquel was working well for the perpetrator. The prosecutor pointed out that while the killer may be on this drug, it is not a miracle drug that we can rely on to keep this man from being violent again. He pointed out that there are guards at the mental health facility and people monitoring the patients, making sure they take the required medications. There is no access to items that could be used as a weapon. It is a controlled environment that is much different than being set free out in the real world.

The judge pulled out some of the letters that people had written him asking for the maximum sentence in this case. He said something to the effect that he does not put much weight on letters he receives. The judge ended up giving Ben's killer 23 years to be served at 100 percent with no possibility of parole. This was two years short of the maximum sentence. Perhaps he felt it was a compromise between not guilty by reason of insanity and first degree murder.

The fact that this man is going to walk free one day concerns me a great deal as I do not believe he will be rehabilitated upon his release. This could prove extremely dangerous to society. If our criminal justice system is truly meant to protect society as a whole, they miserably failed in this case. This man should never be free to harm another innocent person.

Disarming law-abiding citizens IS WRONG. It's wrong and our lawmakers need to be reminded consistently that it's wrong. Every lawmaker in this country took an oath to uphold our constitution. It's our job to make sure they follow through.

CONCLUSION

THE PURPOSE OF SHARING MY EX-
periences with you is my hope that you can learn
something through me and what I have been
through. I don't ever want to see an innocent person become
a victim, because they had no way to defend themselves.
I've been there, done that and I have the T-shirt. Let's face
it, bad guys are going to find a way to get guns. I don't want
criminals to be armed, and we already have plenty of laws
on the books to try and prevent that. The problem is that bad
guys don't follow laws, law-abiding people do. Witnessing
my husband's murder was extremely difficult and it contin-
ues to be a healing process for me. Even after all I have been
through in this nightmare, there is no way I would want to
restrict the rights of good people because of the actions of
one loose cannon with a gun. I don't blame the gun, I blame
the murderer.

It's important that you realize you have the power to stand
up and fight for your constitutional rights and make change
for yourself and others. Don't wait until something horrible
happens to either yourself or a loved one.

Never in my life did I think I would be in this position and writing a book about it. Never did I understand the power of one stubborn individual and the power of more people when they band together. There are those in this world that go along to get along and never make waves when waves are needed, then there are those that have the intestinal fortitude to stand up and bring attention to something that is wrong even if it means being humiliated and discriminated against.

Many wrongs have been made right in this country because of those people. Disarming law-abiding citizens IS WRONG. It's wrong and our lawmakers need to be reminded consistently that it's wrong. Every lawmaker in this country took an oath to uphold our constitution. It's our job to make sure they follow through.

Stand up and refuse to be a victim.

About the Author

Nicole "Nikki" Goeser lives in middle Tennessee and is a graduate of The University of Tennessee Knoxville where she earned her degree in Psychology. Nikki became a Second Amendment Activist after the brutal murder of her husband "Ben" by a man that had been stalking her. She has been featured on programs such as *Nightline*, *Fox Business* with John Stossel, ABC News, CNN, The BBC and NRA News. Nikki was awarded the Sybil Ludington Women's Freedom Award by the National Rifle Association in 2012 for her activism.

4896622R00089

Printed in Great Britain
by Amazon.co.uk, Ltd.,
Marston Gate.